WEATHER

WEATHER

 Reader's Digest

The Reader's Digest Association, Inc.
Pleasantville, New York/Montreal

CONTENTS

WORLD CLIMATIC ZONES 100

FORECASTING THE WEATHER 112

PEOPLE AND WEATHER 136

A Reader's Digest Book

Conceived and produced by Weldon Owen Pty Limited

A member of the Weldon Owen Group of Companies

The credits and acknowledgments that appear on page 160 are hereby made a part of this copyright page.

Copyright 1997 © Weldon Owen Pty Ltd

Printed in China

Weldon Owen Pty Ltd

PUBLISHER: Sheena Coupe

ASSOCIATE PUBLISHER: Lynn Humphries

PROJECT EDITOR: Dawn Titmus

EDITORIAL ASSISTANT: Vesna Radojcic

ART DIRECTOR: Sue Rawkins

DESIGNER: Avril Makula

PICTURE RESEARCHER: Annette Crueger

ILLUSTRATORS: Nick Farmer, Chris Forsey, Robert Hynes

INDEXER: Garry Cousins

PRODUCTION MANAGER: Caroline Webber

AUTHORS: Bruce Buckley (Chapter 3, 7) , John R Colquhoun (Chapter 1), Pat Sullivan (Chapter 2, 5), Richard Whitaker (Chapter 4, 6)

Library of Congress Cataloging in Publication Data Weather
    p. cm. — (Reader's digest explores)
Includes index.
ISBN 0-89577-975-7
1. Weather—Popular works. 2. Climatology—Popular works. 3. Meteorology—Popular works. 4. Reader's Digest Association. I. Series.
QC981.2.W37 1997
551.5—dc21   97-3324

Understanding Weather

The sun's energy drives the enormous waves of air and swirling masses of cloud that surround the earth and create the weather. The earth's inclined axis as it journeys around the sun causes the seasonal cycles, and the seasons and our location determine to a great extent the kind of weather we experience.

WHAT IS WEATHER?

Fluffy, white clouds and clear, blue skies; gale-force winds and torrential rain; golden, fall leaves fringed with frost; dew glistening on a spider's web; terrible twisters spinning a trail of destruction; or the sheer brilliance of lightning erupting across the summer night sky—all these are part of the ever-shifting kaleidoscope of events we call the weather.

WEATHER EVERYWHERE

Although weather is experienced everywhere on earth, it varies considerably from place to place, day to day, and season to season.

From space, the earth looks like a huge, bluish sphere partially covered by large, swirling masses of white clouds. Enormous currents of air, known as global winds, flow around the planet. It's only in the last 200 years or so that we've come to understand how this giant ocean of air, known as the atmosphere (see page 10), works and how the weather is produced.

Natural forces and cycles create the weather, both globally and locally. The primary external force driving the atmosphere is the sun. Solar energy strikes the earth directly in regions close to the Equator and more obliquely at higher latitudes. Thus surface temperatures are higher at the Equator than at the Poles.

The atmosphere constantly tends to smooth out these temperature differences by transporting warm air from the Equator toward the Poles, and moving cold, polar air toward the Equator (see page 22). At the same time, this movement of air is deflected by the earth's rotation. An additional complication is the day–night cycle, which causes one half of the earth to heat up while the other half cools (see page 14).

Other temperature differences, such as those between the air near the ground and that higher up, and between land and sea, are also smoothed out by processes such as convection and land and sea breezes (see pages 12 and 44).

The "engine of weather" can therefore be seen as movements of air tending to equalize differences in temperature across the globe. Equilibrium can never be achieved, however, as long as the sun powers the system, and the atmosphere remains in constant, restless motion with winds continually blowing.

WEATHER AND CLIMATE

While weather is made up of the day-to-day changes in the atmosphere, longer-term variations also occur, and these are collectively known as a region's climate.

When meteorologists (scientists who study the weather) talk about climate, they mention such things as average maximum and minimum temperatures, average humidities, and average rainfall. These averages are usually assembled in monthly blocks, and generally have to be collected for at least 30 years to present an accurate climatic picture.

Climate is more than averages, though; extremes and the frequency of events between them are also important. For example, engineers designing large dams need to know the highest likely rainfall rate over the catchment area so they can produce the safest spillway design. And in designing urban drainage systems, engineers often consider the rainfall rates that can be expected once every 100 years.

Recently a great deal of detective work—using natural records such as growth patterns in trees and coral, as well as fossil evidence (see page 138)—has gone into studying past climates of the earth.

RIGHT: Weather ranges from the destructive power of a wildfire in summer to the natural beauty of a winter's day, such as these icicles reflecting the sun's rays, left inset, or delicate frost patterns on fallen leaves, right inset.

BELOW: Mist floats over a glassy lake on a cold winter's day in Asheville, North Carolina.

OUR OCEAN OF AIR: THE ATMOSPHERE

The earth is surrounded by a thin layer of gases, called the atmosphere, which is held in place by gravity. The atmosphere is vitally important because it allows life on earth to exist: it provides the oxygen we and many other living things need to breathe and protects us from the sun's harmful radiation. It is also the arena for the world's weather.

ATMOSPHERIC LAYERS
The atmosphere is very thin. If the earth were the size of an onion, for instance, the atmosphere would be only about as thick as the skin. Thanks to scientific experiments, starting with explorations by hot-air balloonists in the 18th century, we now know that the atmosphere is divided into five layers. The first layer, which extends to about 6 miles (10 km) above the earth's surface, is called the troposphere. In this layer the atmospheric temperature decreases with altitude: on average by about 4°F every 1,000 feet (7°C/km).

The troposphere—the air we breathe—is composed mainly of nitrogen and oxygen, with small amounts of water vapor (water in a gaseous form), argon, carbon dioxide, and other gases. The water vapor in the troposphere is responsible for much of the weather we experience, and it's in this layer that most of the earth's weather takes place.

The top of the troposphere tends to limit the height of clouds, but very severe thunderstorms, called supercells (see page 49), may "overshoot the top" and extend upward into the next layer, the stratosphere.

The temperature increases to about 27°F (−3°C) in the stratosphere, which extends from 6 to 30 miles (10 to 50 km) above the surface. The ozone layer is located in this layer (see page 144), and is very important for shielding the earth from the sun's harmful ultraviolet (UV) rays.

The temperature falls to about minus 130°F (−90°C) in the next layer, the mesosphere, which occurs at an altitude of about 30 to 50 miles (50 to 80 km).

Above this layer is the thermosphere, at approximately 50 to 310 miles (80 to 500 km) above the surface. Here the temperatures range

LEFT: This picture of cumulus clouds (see page 42) over the Pacific Ocean was taken by the crew of the Space Shuttle Atlantis in 1992. The clouds were produced by a frontal system (see page 26) off the West Coast of the United States.

between minus 130°F and 3,000°F (−90°C and 1,650°C). The thermosphere is the first line of defense against such hazards as meteors and discarded satellites, because the very high temperatures produced by friction with the air burn up most objects heading toward earth.

Between each of these four layers there is little change in temperature; these "mini-layers" are called the tropopause, stratopause, and mesopause. The top layer of the atmosphere, above about 310 miles (500 km), is the exosphere. Beyond the exosphere is what we refer to as "space."

OBSERVING THE ATMOSPHERE
We have moved a long way from exploring the atmosphere with kites or hot-air balloons (see pages 120 and 121). Today meteorologists use many different observing methods. Satellites orbiting the earth far above the surface (see page 122) transmit information about winds, clouds, ground temperatures, and ocean waves. Radar (see page 122) measures winds and rainfall and tracks the course of storms. Weather balloons (see page 124) take electronic instruments high into the atmosphere and transmit readings to ground stations. All these methods allow us to form a detailed picture of the earth's atmosphere and how it affects the weather.

BELOW: Hot-air ballooning is now mostly a leisure-time activity, but in the 18th and 19th centuries it was the only way for people to explore the upper atmosphere.

BELOW: *This massive cumulonimbus cloud (see page 42) has grown to the top of the troposphere. A rain shower is falling from the base of the cloud.*

ATMOSPHERIC LAYERS

The heights of the layers are approximate and vary considerably with latitude and season. The proportions of the layers are distorted for this illustration.

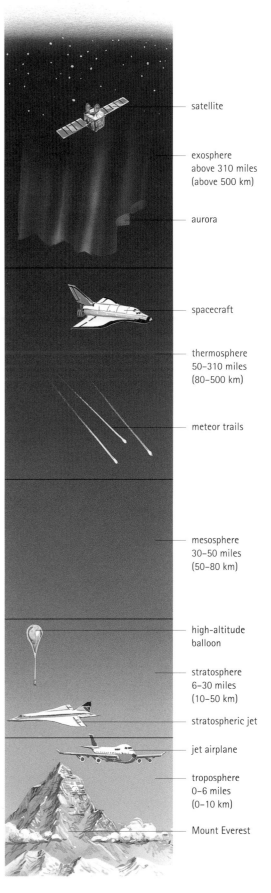

satellite

exosphere
above 310 miles
(above 500 km)

aurora

spacecraft

thermosphere
50–310 miles
(80–500 km)

meteor trails

mesosphere
30–50 miles
(50–80 km)

high-altitude
balloon

stratosphere
6–30 miles
(10–50 km)

stratospheric jet

jet airplane

troposphere
0–6 miles
(0–10 km)

Mount Everest

THE ENGINE OF WEATHER

The sun is the driving force behind our weather on earth. It heats some areas of the earth more than others (see page 8), and land and water respond differently to the sun's rays. Water needs more heat than most solids before it reaches the same temperature. Because of this the ocean warms more slowly than land during the day. At night the situation is reversed and the ocean cools more slowly than land. Because the air above land and sea have different temperatures, there are corresponding differences in air pressure all over the globe. These are the cause of winds (see page 44). Certain mechanisms cause air to rise and cool, which lead to the formation of clouds and precipitation—that is, rain, hail, or snow (see pages 40, 46, and 54).

CONVECTION AND AIR PRESSURE

Even though air is invisible, it's composed of billions of molecules and has weight. The more molecules of air there are above a given point, the more "weight," or pressure, the air has. The unit of measurement for air pressure is the hectopascal (an alternative is the millibar). At sea level the pressure is about 1,010 hectopascals, but air pressure decreases the higher you go. If you climb up a high mountain, for instance, you'll find it more difficult to breathe because there is less air density than at sea level, which means you inhale fewer oxygen molecules.

Air molecules are constantly moving around, and the air temperature affects how quickly they move. Heat makes the molecules in a parcel of air move faster, causing it to expand. You can test this by blowing up a party balloon and then gently heating it (by leaving it in the sun, for example). You'll see that after a short time the balloon becomes larger because the heated air inside is expanding. If you heat some air, it becomes lighter, or more buoyant, than the surrounding air and rises. This process is known as convection. If you cool air, by contrast, it becomes heavier, or denser, than the surrounding air and sinks.

There is an intimate connection between air temperature and air pressure. In summer air over land is heated, becomes buoyant, and rises, creating low pressure. In winter the reverse process occurs: air over land is cooled, becomes denser, and sinks, creating high pressure (see page 28).

CONVECTION

Convection occurs when air heated at ground level rises and cools. When the air temperature falls to the point where its water vapor condenses (becomes liquid), clouds form (see page 40).

LEFT: Although high-pressure cells are usually associated with fine and settled weather and clear skies, clouds do sometimes form, such the cumulus clouds pictured here. However, such clouds are not usually thick enough to produce precipitation.

An area of high pressure is called a high, or anticyclone, and an area of low pressure is called a low, or cyclone. The air rising in a low-pressure cell is cooled as it rises. Usually its temperature falls to the point where water vapor condenses and clouds form (see page 40). This process often goes hand in hand with convection. With a high-pressure cell the reverse occurs: sinking air is warmed as it sinks, so few or no clouds form. Put simply, low-pressure areas are usually associated with cloudy skies, and high-pressure areas are usually associated with relatively clear skies.

WINDY WEATHER

Natural forces are always seeking to smooth out differences in temperature or pressure. So if a region has a low-pressure area, air will rush in from a nearby high-pressure area to fill the "gap." This movement of air is what we know as wind. The larger the differences in pressure between areas, the stronger the winds will be.

The earth's rotation also affects the direction in which the winds blow (see page 24). In the Northern Hemisphere winds are deflected to the right, and in the Southern Hemisphere they are deflected to the left.

BELOW: The sun's interaction with the atmosphere and the surface of the earth is the engine of weather. The setting sun has tinged these altocumulus clouds a golden pink at Port Hedland, in Western Australia.

THE SEASONS

Everywhere on the earth the weather varies to a greater or lesser extent throughout the year. These different weather patterns are known as seasons. What creates the seasons is the combination of the earth's tilt and its orbit around the sun.

THE EARTH'S ORBIT

The distance between the earth and the sun is about 93 million miles (149 million km). The earth rotates around the sun in an elliptical, or oval-shaped, path and takes about 365 days, or one year, to complete an orbit.

The earth also rotates in a counterclockwise direction about its north–south axis, an imaginary line that runs between the Poles. It takes about 24 hours for the earth to spin around once, and this rotation creates day and night. When one half of the world is in darkness, the other half is in daylight.

The earth is also tilted about 23.5° on its axis. So depending on the time of year, certain latitudes of the earth incline toward the sun more than others. Throughout the year different areas, particularly those that are far from the Equator, receive more or less solar radiation. If the earth didn't tilt, we wouldn't have seasons.

For about six months every year the North Pole is closer to the sun than the South Pole is. When the Northern Hemisphere reaches its greatest inclination toward the sun, the area north of the Tropic of Cancer (23.5°N) receives its maximum solar radiation, and days are long—it's summer. As the earth continues on its orbit, the North Pole begins to tilt away from the sun. By December the North Pole is farthest from the sun, temperatures in the Northern Hemisphere are near their lowest, and days are short—it's winter.

When it's summer in the Northern Hemisphere, it's winter in the south, and when it's spring in the Northern Hemisphere, it's fall in the south, and so on.

SOLSTICES AND EQUINOXES

The longest day, or summer solstice, in the Northern Hemisphere occurs about June 22. At this time the sun is directly above the Tropic of Cancer and is at its highest in the sky north of this latitude. Areas north of the Arctic Circle (66.5°N) experience 24 hours of daylight (known as the midnight sun) for up to six months. The shortest day, or winter solstice, occurs about December 22, when the sun is lowest in the sky. At this time areas north of the Arctic Circle undergo 24 hours of darkness for months.

There are two days in the year, called the spring and autumnal equinoxes, when night and day have an equal length of 12 hours almost all over the world. The spring equinox occurs in March in the Northern Hemisphere and in September in the south, while the autumnal equinox occurs in September in the north and in March in the south. On these days the sun is directly over the Equator, and the sun rises almost exactly in the east and sets almost exactly in the west over the entire earth.

SEASONAL VARIETY

Because of the earth's spherical shape, the sun's rays strike parts of the earth at greater or lesser angles, heating some areas more than others. Equatorial regions are heated most and remain hot all year long, while the Poles are heated least and stay cold throughout the year.

Most of the areas in between are temperate regions (see page 18), which are generally hot in summer and cold in winter, and have distinct seasons: spring, summer, fall, and winter. Tropical regions, between the tropics of Cancer and Capricorn, have wet and dry seasons but experience little temperature change over the course of a year (see page 70).

RIGHT: Temperate regions exhibit great seasonal variations and temperature changes over a year. These four landscapes illustrate the four different seasons in various areas of the United States (clockwise from top left): maple trees in fall, Utah; a winter scene in Connecticut; the Texas prairie in spring; and summer wildflowers in the Colorado Rocky Mountains.

THE EARTH'S ORBIT

During summer in the Northern Hemisphere the longest day (the summer solstice) occurs when the sun is directly over the Tropic of Cancer. As the earth continues its year-long orbit, the North Pole tilts away from the sun, and the South Pole tilts toward the sun. The equinoxes occur when the sun is directly over the Equator; on these days there are 12 hours of daylight and 12 hours of darkness over almost the entire world. The Northern Hemisphere winter solstice (the shortest day) occurs when the sun is over the Tropic of Capricorn.

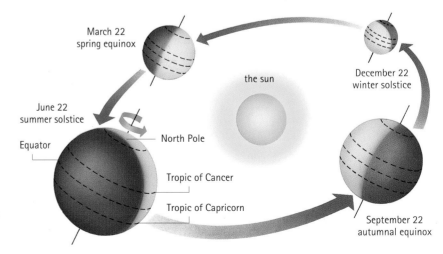

March 22
spring equinox

December 22
winter solstice

June 22
summer solstice

the sun

Equator

North Pole

Tropic of Cancer

Tropic of Capricorn

September 22
autumnal equinox

THE EARTH'S CLIMATE

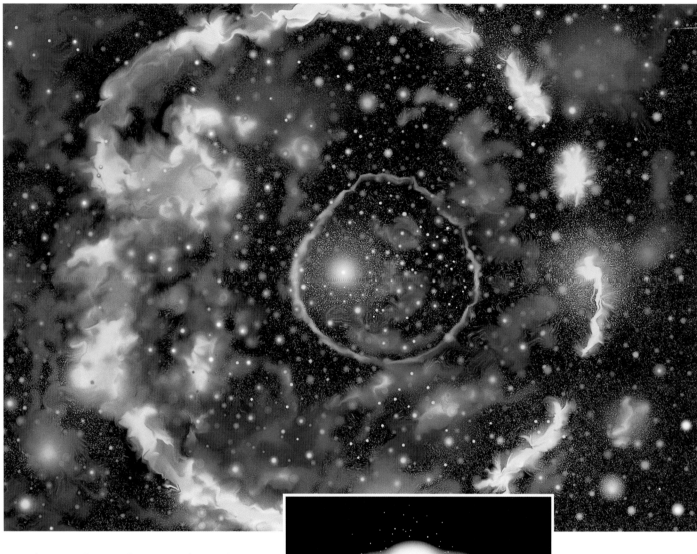

As far as we know, changes in the earth's climate have occurred throughout the planet's history. Scientists estimate that the earth formed about 4,600 million years ago, and although we have some clues to the earth's "recent" history—that is, from about a million years ago—we know very little about the climate before then (see page 138).

ICE AGES

One thing we do know is that the earth has experienced a number of ice ages, many severe and long-lasting, when huge ice sheets and glaciers covered large parts of the land and conditions were extremely cold. The end of the last ice age is thought to have occurred about 10,000 years ago. During this time ice sheets covered much of North America, all of Scandinavia, and the northern half of the British Isles. The oceans were about 400 feet (120 m) lower than they are today. Before this, for hundreds of thousands of years, the earth was thought to have been mostly cooler than now, with average global temperatures varying by 9°F to 12°F (5°C to 7°C).

Since the last ice age the climate has been more stable and average global temperatures have varied by less than 4°F (2°C). There was a period from 1450 to 1850, called the little

ABOVE AND INSET: Although we cannot be certain what our galaxy, the Milky Way, looks like, these illustrations depict how scientists believe the center, above, and profile, inset, would appear. Some scientists believe the Milky Way may affect the earth's climate. The earth passes through dust lanes on the outer edges of the galaxy every 150 million years. It's thought the dust may block out some of the sunlight that normally would reach earth.

ABOVE: *This image of the earth is a composite photograph taken from a polar-orbiting satellite about 530 miles (860 km) above the earth's surface. Part of southern Africa and Madagascar are visible, while bands of cloud spiral over the Southern Ocean and Antarctica.*

THE MILANKOVITCH THEORY

1 The earth is currently tilted on its vertical axis (an imaginary line that runs between the Poles) at an angle of 23.5°. Milankovitch argued the earth's tilt varies between 21.8° and 24.4° every 41,000 years.

2 The earth's orbit becomes more and less elliptical every 100,000 and 43,000 years.

ice age, when temperatures were about 2°F (1°C) lower than now. Glaciers were extensive in most alpine areas and normally free-flowing rivers such as London's River Thames often froze over in winter.

WHY DOES THE CLIMATE CHANGE?

Researchers have put forward numerous theories about why the earth's climate fluctuates. In the 1930s a Yugoslav scientist called Milutin Milankovitch proposed a theory that long-term climate change is due to variations in the earth's tilt and orbit, and the time of year when the earth is closest to the sun.

Milankovitch argued that the earth's tilt varies from 21.8° to 24.4° every 41,000 years. A large tilt produces big seasonal changes in temperature outside tropical areas, causing ice sheets to melt, while a small tilt minimizes temperature variations, allowing ice sheets to grow.

Milankovitch concluded that the earth's orbit of the sun becomes more and less elliptical every

100,000 and 43,000 years, and that the time of year when the earth is closest to the sun fluctuates every 23,000 years. Scientists believe these factors affect the intensity of solar radiation that different parts of the earth receive, which at times leads to lower temperatures and ice ages.

Other theories put forward to explain climate change are that the amount of solar radiation varies, usually in 11-year cycles, and that as the continents, which once formed one large landmass, have split up and drifted from their initial positions, the climate has changed.

Volcanic eruptions also affect climate: in June 1991 the eruption of Mount Pinatubo, in the Philippines, sent huge numbers of tiny particles, called aerosols, high into the stratosphere. Average surface temperatures fell by about 1°F (0.6°C) over the next 12 months.

Temperatures at the ocean surface are very important in determining day-to-day weather. Scientists believe variations in the circulation of water in the oceans, known as the great ocean conveyor belt (see page 36), may cause changes in the climate many years later.

Since about 1900 temperatures over the globe have increased by 0.5°F to 1°F (0.3°C to 0.6°C) and many scientists believe this increase is due to the higher concentrations of greenhouse gases in the atmosphere (see page 140).

24.4°
23.5°
21.8°

2

1

ABOVE: *Mount Augustine volcano, Alaska. Volcanic eruptions can affect the earth's climate as minute particles in the atmosphere reduce the amount of solar radiation reaching earth.*

WORLD CLIMATIC ZONES

The world is made up of a number of climatic zones, each of which is influenced by such factors as latitude, altitude, average annual amount and strength of sunlight, oceans and their currents, mountains, global winds, and prevailing local winds.

CLASSIFYING CLIMATES

One very simple way to classify climates is to consider whether a region is continental (inland) or maritime (on or near the coast). The interior of North America can be classified as a continental climate, for example, while areas on the seaboard have a maritime climate. Most islands have a maritime climate, though the larger ones, such as Australia, may have a continental climate away from the coast.

More complex climate classification systems consider average temperature, humidity, and rainfall, and analyze how these vary during the year. In some locations the main type of vegetation is also a factor; for example, whether it is rain forest or grasslands. If we consider all these variables, the climatic zones of the world can be classified as polar and subarctic, tropical and subtropical, temperate, mountain, arid and semi-arid, and Mediterranean. See the chapter "World Climatic Zones" on pages 100–11.

ZONES AROUND THE WORLD

The Poles receive less and weaker sunlight than anywhere else on earth, so these regions experience relatively low temperatures all year round. Snow and ice cover the ground for all

BELOW: *Joshua trees, such as these in California's Mojave Desert, are adapted to the arid and semi-arid regions of the American Southwest.*

LEFT: Rain forests are found primarily in tropical and subtropical zones. The high rainfall and humidity of these areas provide ideal conditions for lush vegetation to grow.

RIGHT: A caribou bull stands with its impressive semi-circular antlers silhouetted against Mount McKinley in Denali National Park, Alaska. Caribou are among the very few large grazing mammals inhabiting subarctic regions.

CLIMATIC ZONES
- Tropical savanna
- Tropical rain forest
- Subtropical
- Arid
- Semi-arid
- Temperate
- Subarctic
- Mountain
- Mediterranean
- Polar

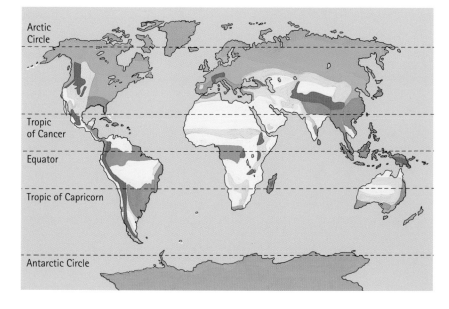

or most of the year. Polar regions lie mostly north of the Arctic Circle and south of the Antarctic Circle (see map below) and are also known as the high latitudes. The subarctic region lies south of the Arctic polar zone. The climate here is similar to that in temperate zones but winters are much colder and longer. There is no equivalent zone in the Southern Hemisphere because there are no significant landmasses just north of the Antarctic Circle.

Between the Arctic and Antarctic circles and the tropics of Cancer and Capricorn lie the middle latitudes. Parts of this area have a temperate climate but there are many variations. Temperate zones typically have cold winters, warm summers, and fairly predictable rainfall patterns from year to year.

Some regions in the mid-latitudes, such as parts of California and southern Australia, have Mediterranean climates with cool, wet winters and hot, dry summers.

The region lying between the two tropics, known as the low latitudes, generally has either a tropical or subtropical climate with distinct wet and dry seasons. The tropical zone can be subdivided into tropical rain forests and tropical savannas. Temperature, rainfall, and humidity are high in both, but in rain-forest areas the dry season is short, while in savanna regions the wet and dry seasons are of equal length.

Arid and semi-arid zones exist in both the low and mid-latitudes. In arid zones there is a large difference between daytime and night-time temperatures, and it rarely rains. Semi-arid zones have slightly more rainfall, and the difference between day- and night-time temperatures is not so extreme.

Mountainous zones are also found in low and mid-latitudes. Temperatures are much lower than at places nearer sea level at similar latitudes. For example, in the high, mountainous areas of Mount Kenya, in Africa, which is almost on the Equator, temperatures are typical of the cold regions of the high latitudes.

SULTRY DAYS: TEMPERATURE AND HUMIDITY

People react differently to the amount of heat in the atmosphere, which is defined as temperature. Weather that might be considered cold to people living in the tropics could be deemed a heatwave by residents of polar regions. How hot or cold we feel is a matter not only of perception but also of such physical factors as humidity and wind speed.

TEMPERATURE SCALES

Two scales are used to measure temperature. The Celsius, or centigrade, scale is the official scale in most countries, but the Fahrenheit scale is still used in the United States and Britain. German scientist Gabriel Fahrenheit (1686–1736) introduced the Fahrenheit scale in 1714. The major points of his scale were 0°F, which was the lowest temperature people could produce then, and 96°F, which Fahrenheit assumed to be the temperature of the human body. On this scale the freezing point of water is 32°F and its boiling point is 212°F.

The Swedish astronomer Anders Celsius (1701–44) developed his scale in 1742. This is based on two fixed points, the freezing (0°C)

and boiling points (100°C) of water, with the scale divided into 100 equal parts between these two points.

The formula to convert °F to °C is: $(°F - 32) \times \frac{5}{9}$. The formula to convert °C to °F is: $(°C \times \frac{9}{5}) + 32$.

MEASURING THE HUMIDITY

Meteorologists use the term *humidity* to describe the quantity of water vapor in the air. The temperature of the air determines the amount of water vapor it can hold: the warmer the air, the more water vapor. When air can hold no more water vapor, it's said to be saturated. The temperature at which saturation occurs is known as the dewpoint temperature (see page 40). At the dewpoint water vapor will start to become liquid, or condense.

There are two ways of expressing humidity: absolute and relative humidity. Absolute humidity is a measure of the mass of water in a given volume of air at the current temperature. Relative humidity is a measure of the amount of water vapor in the air relative to the amount needed to saturate the air at that temperature.

ABOVE: *This French thermometer, dating from the late 18th century, is calibrated to the Celsius scale. There is a common temperature on the Celsius and Fahrenheit scales at 40° below zero.*

LEFT: *Tropical rain forests such as this one in Brazil have distinct wet and dry seasons, but they are humid all year round. Recent rains have flooded part of the forest.*

ABOVE: Poppies carpet part of the Mojave Desert, in California, after spring rains. The flowers will set seed for next year's crop in just a few days, then wither and die as the soil's moisture evaporates with rising temperatures. Humidity is usually low in arid regions, so temperatures can seem lower than they actually are because perspiration evaporates rapidly from our skin, cooling us down.

So if the relative humidity is 50 percent, the air is holding half its capacity of water vapor. If the air temperature were to rise, the relative humidity would decrease because warmer air can hold more water vapor.

Relative humidity can be measured by comparing the temperatures of wet-bulb and dry-bulb thermometers (see page 124). The wet-bulb thermometer is surrounded by wet muslin and measures the temperature of the saturated air, while the dry bulb measures the actual air temperature. If both thermometers indicate the same temperature, then the air has a relative humidity of 100 percent.

Measurements can also be made electronically, and this is the method employed in many automatic weather stations (see page 124).

Human hair can be a good indicator of humidity: curly hair becomes straighter when the air is humid. Early hygrometers utilized treated human hair to measure humidity, and it's still used in the hair hygrometer (see page 124).

One effect of high humidity is to make it feel hotter than it actually is. In very humid regions we feel uncomfortably hot because perspiration evaporates from our skin slowly, and as a result our bodies do not lose very much heat.

GLOBAL WINDS

The sun heats some areas of the earth more than others, and the differences in temperature lead to the formation of winds (see page 44). The major wind flows over the earth can be described as the general circulation of the atmosphere, or global wind patterns.

In each hemisphere there are three vertical circulations of air: the Hadley cell, which circulates between the Equator and 30°N and S; the Ferrel cell, which occurs from 30 to 60°N and S; and the polar cell, which lies between the Poles and 60°N and S (see illustration below).

THE HADLEY CELLS

In 1753 English scientist George Hadley (1686–1768) first described the circulation of air in the tropics to explain, in part, the trade winds. Tropical regions receive more intense levels of sunlight than other regions of the earth. The sun's radiation produces powerful convection currents (see page 12), enhancing low-pressure areas near the Equator. As the warm, humid air rises, clouds and frequent thunderstorms form.

The rising air eventually meets the top of the troposphere, where it spreads out toward the Poles, cools, and sinks at about 30° north and south of the Equator. The sinking air creates a high-pressure area, which is generally associated with warm, settled weather, and this is where most of the world's deserts are located. Some of this air then moves back toward the low-pressure area near the Equator. The air flow is known as the northeast trade winds in the Northern Hemisphere and the southeast trade winds in the Southern Hemisphere.

The high-pressure belts at 30°N and S are also areas of light winds. They became known as the horse latitudes in the Atlantic, because

when water supplies ran low, mariners used to throw their cargo of horses overboard from sailing ships that were making slow progress.

Besides the intense solar radiation in equatorial regions, another reason for the frequent thunderstorms here is the meeting, or convergence, of the trade winds, which causes the low-level air to ascend.

The area where the trade winds from the two hemispheres meet used to be known as the doldrums, from an old English word meaning *dull*, because of the light winds that usually prevailed. In the days of sailing ships, mariners feared being stranded there. Today meteorologists refer to this area as the intertropical convergence zone (ITCZ). Its location shifts every six months from one hemisphere to the other, usually settling in the summer hemisphere. This warm, humid zone is where hurricanes are likely to form (see page 66).

RIGHT: A blizzard at Waterton Lakes National Park, Alberta, Canada, located at about 49°N. Gale-force winds are common around the 40° to 50° latitudes. The US National Weather Service defines a blizzard as a considerable falling or blowing of snow, with winds of 35 miles per hour (56 km/h) or more. Temperatures may be 10°F (–12°C) or lower.

GLOBAL WINDS

There are three major vertical circulations of air in each hemisphere: the Hadley cell, the Ferrel cell, and the polar cell. The earth's rotation affects wind direction. In the Northern Hemisphere surface air in the Hadley cell is deflected to the right as it returns to the Equator, forming northeast trade winds. In the Southern Hemisphere the air is deflected to the left, forming southeast trade winds.

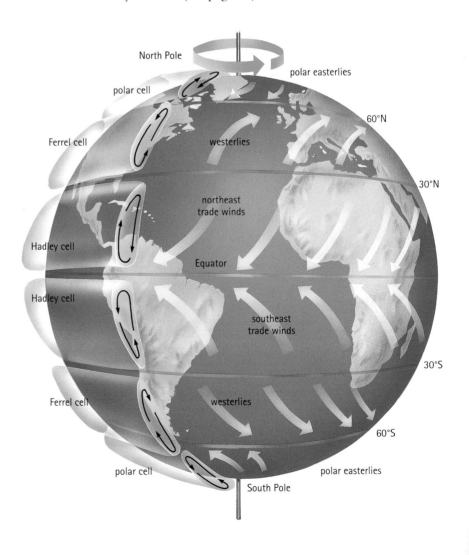

North Pole

polar easterlies

polar cell

Ferrel cell

60°N

westerlies

30°N

northeast trade winds

Hadley cell

Equator

Hadley cell

southeast trade winds

30°S

Ferrel cell

westerlies

60°S

polar cell

polar easterlies

South Pole

THE FERREL AND POLAR CELLS

Some air from the descending part of the Hadley cell flows toward the Poles and forms the surface part of the Ferrel cell. This was first described in 1856 by American meteorologist William Ferrel (1817–91). Some of the cool air rises at about 60°N and S, where low-pressure centers are frequent.

In both hemispheres westerly surface winds are common in the 40° latitudes, particularly in winter. The westerlies develop on the equatorward side of the deep low-pressure centers. In the era of sail, these latitudes were known as the roaring 40s in the Southern Hemisphere because of the frequent gale-force westerlies. Nowadays sailors in round-the-world yacht races take advantage of the windy conditions to speed their progress across the Southern Ocean, although sometimes these strong winds can be hazardous, rather than helpful, to sailors.

Cold, polar air sinks and flows away from the Poles at the surface, forming the downward branch of the polar cells. The surface air in the polar cells meets the surface air in the Ferrel cells at about the 60° latitudes.

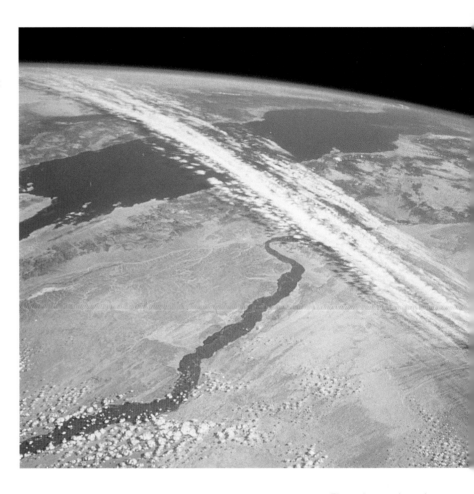

ABOVE: These elongated streaks of cirrus cloud indicate a jet stream racing across Egypt and the Red Sea from west to east. The River Nile extends from the lower left.

THE CORIOLIS EFFECT

The rotation of the earth causes moving objects, such as winds and ocean currents, to be deflected from their original direction. In the Northern Hemisphere the deviation is to the right along the direction of travel, and in the Southern Hemisphere it's to the left. There is no deviation at the Equator and the effect is most pronounced at the Poles.

The Coriolis effect, as it's known, is named after French physicist Gustave-Gaspard de Coriolis (1792–1843), who first identified it in 1835. It not only affects wind direction, but also causes air to rotate around low- and high-pressure centers and affects the direction of this rotation (see page 28). For example, winds rotate clockwise around high-pressure systems in the Northern Hemisphere, and counterclockwise in the Southern Hemisphere. Winds rotate in the opposite directions around low-pressure systems.

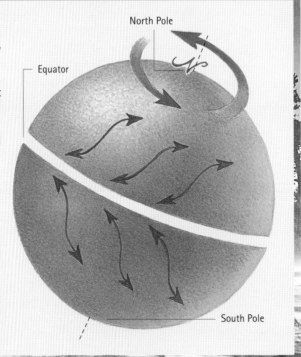

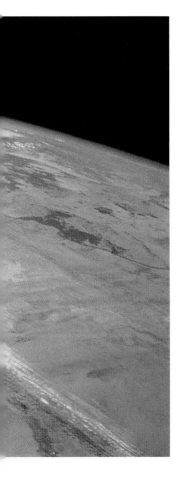

The circulation in the Ferrel and polar cells is much weaker than that of the tropical Hadley cells. This is because the intense solar radiation in equatorial regions produces strong upward movements of air, known as convection (see page 12). Solar radiation and convection are not as intense at the latitudes where air in the Ferrel and polar cells ascends.

JET STREAMS

Two rapidly moving streams of air in each hemisphere, known as jet streams, often snake through the upper parts of the troposphere. Predominantly westerly winds, they are caused by strong temperature and pressure changes in this part of the atmosphere. They can be thousands of miles long, hundreds of miles wide, and a mile or two deep.

Long lines of cloud high in the sky often indicate the presence of a jet stream. The cloud forms when air moves upward and rotates around the jet stream.

Their positions are constantly shifting, but in general jet streams coincide with the meeting points of the Hadley and Ferrel cells (the subtropical jet), and the Ferrel and polar cells (the polar-front jet).

The subtropical jet is the most intense, occasionally reaching speeds of about 300 miles per hour (500 km/h). It's located on the pole-ward side of the Hadley cell at a height of about 7 miles (12 km). The polar-front jet lies between the polar and Ferrel cells at about 3 to 5 miles (5 to 8 km) above the earth's surface.

Between the two world wars (1918–39), balloon explorations of the atmosphere confirmed the existence of jet streams. Before that, meteorologists had only suspected their presence from observing cloud patterns. Observations of upper winds during World War II (1939–45) produced the data needed for more detailed study.

Since then, the development of weather-balloon and radar networks (see pages 122–4) has revealed the importance of jet streams to the evolution of weather systems. For instance, they can have a crucial role in the development of low-pressure systems, mountain waves, and tornadoes (see pages 26, 32, and 62).

A knowledge of the location and strength of jet streams is important to the aviation industry. Pilots can "hitch a ride" on a jet stream, thereby reducing flight time and saving fuel. If an airplane is traveling in the opposite direction to a jet stream, the pilot can reduce the stream's effect on the aircraft by flying at an altitude where the wind speed is lower.

Wind speeds fluctuate rapidly at the margins of jet streams, resulting in clear-air turbulence that can cause discomfort or even injury to aircraft passengers and crew. Weather services produce forecasts to reduce turbulence hazards.

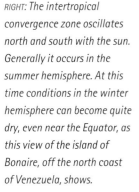

RIGHT: The intertropical convergence zone oscillates north and south with the sun. Generally it occurs in the summer hemisphere. At this time conditions in the winter hemisphere can become quite dry, even near the Equator, as this view of the island of Bonaire, off the north coast of Venezuela, shows.

HARBINGERS OF CHANGE: FRONTAL SYSTEMS

From 1918 to 1923 a team of meteorologists based in Bergen, Norway, and headed by Vilhelm Bjerknes (1862-1951), led the way in modern meteorology. Called the Bergen School, the team made several major theoretical advances in meteorology, one of the most important of which is the theory of fronts, or frontal systems.

AIR MASSES

An air mass is a body of air in which the temperature and humidity remain constant. Air masses can range from thousands of square miles to only a few miles across. The general circulation of the atmosphere moves air masses around, and they can travel large distances.

The Bergen School put forward the idea that most weather is concentrated in comparatively narrow bands between air masses. It called these areas fronts, after the battle zones of World War I (1914–18).

Fronts are the boundaries between warm and cold air masses, and are therefore the agents of change in the weather. They are the zones where the atmosphere is at its most active, at least in the mid- and high latitudes.

There are two main types of fronts, warm and cold, which are common in mid- and high latitudes. They rarely occur in the tropics, because differences between the temperatures of tropical air masses are minor. Warm, moist air dominates the region near the Equator almost permanently.

COLD FRONTS

A cold front occurs when a moving cold air mass displaces an existing warmer air mass by driving like a wedge underneath it (see illustration opposite left). This causes the warmer air to ride up and over the advancing cold air. Cold air masses may move either quite slowly, or very rapidly at speeds of about 60 miles per hour (100 km/h).

The arrival of a cold front usually causes a sudden change in the local weather. Because rising air is a basic ingredient in cloud formation (see page 40), there's usually an increase in clouds, particularly cumuliform clouds (see page 42). Showers, snow, or even thunderstorms can form if the updrafts are strong enough. Temperatures can fall abruptly at the surface, and sudden changes in wind speed and direction also occur at about the same time.

Weather satellites enable meteorologists to track cold fronts from space. They often appear as long, narrow bands of clouds, sometimes extending hundreds of miles across the sky, confirming the theory of the Bergen School.

WARM FRONTS

A warm front occurs when a moving warm air mass meets a colder air mass. The warm air rises over the retreating colder air mass and replaces it at ground level (see illustration opposite right). This leads to an increase in temperature at the surface and a build-up of mainly stratiform clouds.

Compared to cold fronts, warm fronts are normally not as vigorous, nor as fast moving. Because they usually produce stratiform clouds, extensive bands of rain and drizzle develop, rather than the showers and storms that cold fronts generate. Warm fronts may even engender snow if the temperature at the surface is below freezing (32°F/0°C).

Warm fronts occur more frequently in high latitudes than they do in mid-latitudes because large, slow-moving, cold air masses are more common in the high latitudes.

From space warm fronts appear as large, sometimes ill-defined areas of clouds. They tend to be more extensive than the narrow bands associated with cold fronts.

ABOVE: An approaching cold front in Bryce Canyon National Park, Utah. Cold fronts often produce local showers and thunderstorms.

LEFT: Dramatic storm clouds associated with a cold front race over the Southern Ocean.

THE VIEW FROM SPACE

This photograph of the globe was taken from a geostationary satellite about 22,300 miles (35,900 km) above the earth. It shows a cold front moving across southern parts of South America. Such fronts are very common over these latitudes, and often move rapidly from west to east, particularly during winter.

WARM AND COLD FRONTS

A cold front, left, occurs when a mass of cold air drives into a warm air mass. The warm air rises and forms cumuliform clouds. A warm front, right, forms when warm air rides over the top of a mass of cold air, resulting in stratiform clouds.

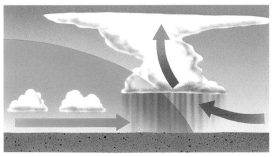

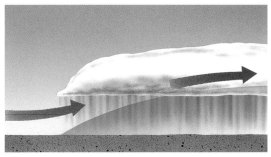

THE HIGHS AND LOWS OF AIR PRESSURE

As we go about our everyday business, we carry a large weight with us. This is the weight of the atmosphere above us pushing on the earth. When it's measured over a particular area, it's called air pressure (see page 12).

TROUGHS AND CRESTS OF AIR

It was the French scientist Blaise Pascal (see page 118) who discovered that air pressure varied considerably from day to day, and that these changes could be related to the weather itself. Pascal put forward the theory that troughs and crests of air move through the atmosphere above us. When a crest is overhead, the air pressure is at a maximum. And when a trough is overhead, the air pressure is at a minimum.

Pascal's theory led to the concept of high- and low-pressure areas in the atmosphere. In the late 17th century meteorologists began a systematic investigation of the effect of air pressure on the weather. Today we know that high- and low-pressure cells naturally form and dissipate in the atmosphere in response to a highly complex series of events. These include the sun's heating of the atmosphere, the rotation of the earth, and the interaction of the atmosphere with landmasses and the oceans.

Areas of high and low air pressure play a large part in determining the weather, and they also have characteristic structures. The identification and monitoring of highs and lows are, therefore, fundamental to accurate weather forecasting. In general highs, also known as anticyclones, are areas where dense air is sinking, and are associated with fair weather. Lows, also known as cyclones, are areas where buoyant air is rising, and are associated with cloudy or rainy weather.

HIGHS AND LOWS

High-pressure cells, which may be several hundred miles across, are large eddies of air that extend to the top of the troposphere, about 6 miles (10 km) above the surface. They rotate clockwise in the Northern Hemisphere, and counterclockwise in the Southern Hemisphere (see illustration opposite top). They are the crests of the atmosphere, and the air pressure underneath the central area is high.

LOW-PRESSURE SYSTEM

When two air masses of different temperatures meet, a low-pressure cell can develop.

1 Over southeast Canada a cold air mass in the west meets a warm air mass in the east.

2 The warm air mass begins to rise over the cold air. An area of low pressure develops.

LEFT: These people on the beach at Damp, in Schleswig Holstein, Germany, are taking advantage of the sea breezes (see page 44) to fly their kites. For sea breezes to form, there need to be sunny conditions, which are usually associated with high-pressure cells.

BELOW A thunderstorm over Tucson, Arizona. Thunderstorms usually occur with low-pressure cells because of the rising air produced by lows.

HIGHS AND LOWS IN THE NORTHERN HEMISPHERE

1. Cool, sinking air rotates clockwise around a high-pressure cell. It becomes warmer and spreads out as it sinks.

2. Warm, rising air rotates counterclockwise around a low-pressure cell, becoming cooler as it rises. It converges at low levels and spreads out higher up.

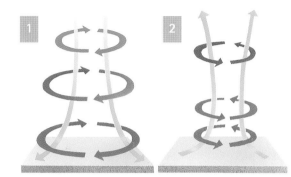

In a high-pressure cell, air aloft gently sinks to the ground. This subsiding air slows down cloud formation, leading to mainly dry weather. Surface winds are usually light, and these tend to spread out from the center of the high. In coastal areas, mainly during summer, sea breezes (see page 44) can form under high-pressure cells, which create more gusty winds, particularly in the afternoon.

With low-pressure cells everything is reversed. Lows are eddies of air that rotate counterclockwise in the Northern Hemisphere, and clockwise in the Southern Hemisphere (see illustration left). They are the atmosphere's troughs, and air pressure under the central area is low. Lows usually extend over a smaller area than do highs.

Air at the surface tends to converge toward the center of the system, rise, and spread out. The rising air produces cloud, which is often accompanied by showers and even thunderstorms. Surface winds tend to increase toward the center of a low and can be strong enough to be gale force.

Lows can be generated by the interaction of warm and cold fronts (see page 26). Highs, on the other hand, are usually associated with single air masses, which can be either warm or cold.

Intense winter highs moving from northwest Canada to the central United States, for instance, create clear skies and light winds. This can result in severe frosts (see page 82), which occasionally extend as far south as Florida and can damage citrus and vegetable crops. Another example is the intense winter high that forms over Siberia, which creates clear skies, light winds, and extremely low overnight temperatures.

3. The rising air causes clouds and precipitation to form. The two air masses begin to rotate.

4. The cold air mass moves faster than the warmer air and begins to catch up with it.

5. The cold air mass catches up with the warmer air, which creates windy, unsettled weather.

6. The cold air cuts off the supply of warm air, and winds and precipitation die down.

WEATHER AND LANDMASSES

Weather is profoundly affected by the interaction of the atmosphere with landmasses. This interaction not only generates local weather, such as cloud and storms, but it also influences broad climatic patterns, such as average rainfall and temperature range.

RAINFALL AND RAIN SHADOWS

When air travels over a landmass, several processes can occur. Air may lose moisture if it mixes with air that has a lower relative humidity (see page 20). It may rise if it meets a barrier such as mountains, leading to cloud and precipitation forming (see page 40). If it's heated by contact with warmer ground, convection (see page 12) may begin, producing clouds and rain.

When moist ocean air flows over land, it generally becomes drier because it mixes with the drier air above it. This effect is minimal over short distances, but air can dry out significantly if it travels over thousands of miles of land. The annual rainfall over a continent generally is highest along the coast and decreases farther inland.

Mountain ranges, which lift air, cause clouds and precipitation. When this happens, the air passing to the leeward sides of the mountains has lost much of its moisture (see illustration above). Thus the windward sides of mountains usually receive regular rains, but the leeward sides get much less. This is known as the rain-shadow effect.

The Rocky Mountains of North America produce a marked rain shadow over areas to the east. Prevailing westerly winds blow across the far southern areas of the Andes mountains in South America. These create a rain shadow in the east, or leeward side, where the desert region of Patagonia is located.

RAIN-SHADOW EFFECT

A mountain range can produce a rain shadow in areas located on the leeward side of the range. Moist air rises on the windward side, where most of the precipitation falls. By the time it crosses the range, the air has become much drier.

RIGHT: Aspen trees in fall create a colorful foreground to Grand Teton, Wyoming. The change of color in the leaves of deciduous trees is triggered by the onset of colder conditions. It occurs earlier in inland areas because of lower overnight temperatures than at the coast.

BELOW: The Namib Desert, in the far southwest of Africa, results from prevailing easterly winds being dried out as they travel over hundreds of miles of land. The stark landscape of sand dunes and scant vegetation is evidence of the very low rainfall in this region.

One of the world's best-defined rain shadows is found at Mandalay, in Burma (Myanmar), which is surrounded on all sides by mountains. Along the coastline to the south annual rainfall is more than 200 inches (5,080 mm), but at Mandalay it's less than 30 inches (762 mm).

One of the driest places on earth is Death Valley, in California. It's surrounded by high ground in all directions, which creates a rain shadow irrespective of wind direction.

LAND AND AIR TEMPERATURE

Compared with the ocean, the surface of the land heats more quickly by day, and cools more quickly by night. This means that inland areas generally have a greater day–night and seasonal temperature range than do coastal regions.

In continental central regions this temperature range can be very large, both over 24 hours and from summer to winter. For example, at Browning, Montana, the temperature fell from 44°F (7°C) to minus 56°F (–49°C) over 24 hours in January 1916.

The largest seasonal variations are usually found in Siberia. Olekminsk, for instance, has recorded a summer high of 113°F (45°C) and a winter low of minus 76°F (–60°C)—a total range of 189°F (105°C)!

Temperature drops with altitude: generally, it will fall by about 11.7°F (6.5°C) with every 3,280-foot (1 km) gain in height. Even near the Equator, where surface temperatures close to sea level are always high, cold conditions can last all year on high mountains. For example, Mount Kilimanjaro, in East Africa close to the Equator, at an altitude of 19,340 feet (5,895 m), has a cap of permanent snow and ice.

LAND, AIR PRESSURE, AND WINDS

Air over inland continental regions is heated and expands during summer, creating low pressure at the surface (see page 28). The hottest parts of these continents have semipermanent heat lows in summer, which often generate afternoon showers and thunderstorms.

The process is reversed in winter. As air near the surface is chilled, high-pressure areas form at the surface. Semipermanent winter highs occur over inland regions of several large

continents. For instance, Siberia has the most intense high-pressure cell in the world, with the central pressure sometimes exceeding 1,060 hectopascals.

Landmasses can affect winds in often quite dramatic ways. When a hurricane makes landfall, for instance, it quickly weakens because it is no longer getting energy from the ocean, and the increased friction with objects on the ground, such as buildings and trees, slows down wind speeds. This is little consolation to coastal communities, which still bear the full brunt of a hurricane, but it does mean that major wind damage doesn't extend far inland. Flooding associated with the weakening hurricane can, however, affect areas a considerable distance inland.

Sea and land breezes (see page 44) result from the interaction of air over land and over sea. And as winds blow over mountain ranges, lenticular, or lens-shaped, clouds (see page 87) may form downwind of the mountains in the crests of waves in the airflow. These waves are known as lee, or mountain, waves.

Raised land can also produce an effect called funneling, in which surface winds speed up when they pass through gaps in hills or mountain ranges (see page 45).

ABOVE: *Fog floats over the Bavarian Forest, in Germany. Inland regions such as this one generally experience lower overnight temperatures than coastal areas, which can mean that fogs are more frequent inland.*

RIGHT: The rainfall over prairie regions in the United States—about 10 to 30 inches (250 to 750 mm)—is too low to support forests but too high to produce desert. Instead, it creates the conditions for large expanses of grassland, and some trees, to grow, such as on this prairie in South Dakota.

LEFT: An elephant in front of a wildfire in northern India. Before the onset of the monsoon (see page 70), the dry vegetation in tropical areas such as this one can lead to frequent wildfires.

WEATHER AND THE OCEANS

What is the link between forest fires in the tropical rain forests of Indonesia, droughts in eastern ,Australia, floods in the deserts of Peru, warmer than usual temperatures over the northeast United States and southern Alaska, and hurricanes in the central South Pacific? The answer is they all occur during an El Niño event (see page 36), and demonstrate the intimate connection between weather and the world's oceans.

THE WATER CYCLE

The oceans cover 70 percent of the globe and contain 97 percent of the earth's water. This seawater is salty and undrinkable. The other 3 percent is fresh water. More than 2 percent of the earth's total water is contained in freshwater ice sheets and glaciers, and less than 1 percent consists of ground water. A small fraction of a percent is contained in lakes, rivers, and the atmosphere. Water is continually being transferred between the oceans, land, plants, and the atmosphere in a process called the water, or hydrologic, cycle (see illustration on page 36).

Most water that's in the atmosphere has evaporated from the oceans. When moist air rises and cools, clouds form (see page 40). Clouds can produce precipitation if they grow sufficiently. Nearly 90 percent of the precipitation that falls over land consists of water that has evaporated from the oceans. Precipitation either soaks into the ground; runs off into lakes, streams, and rivers; or evaporates into the air.

Plants draw water up from the soil via their roots. Eventually, the water passes through the leaves into the air, a process known as transpiration. Water also evaporates from lakes and rivers, falls back to earth as precipitation, and is absorbed by the ground. The water cycle is completed when water returns to the oceans via rivers and underground streams.

ABOVE: The wreck of the cargo ship Ranga *lies off Slea Head, in County Kerry, Ireland. These waters can be several degrees warmer than those of similar latitudes in other parts of the world because of the warming effects of the Gulf Stream in the North Atlantic Ocean.*

RIGHT: Winds, tides, and currents all contribute to the turbulence of the oceans. Stormy winds have whipped up these enormous waves crashing into La Jument lighthouse, off the northwest coast of France.

THE GREAT OCEAN CONVEYOR BELT

In addition to the major ocean currents (see box opposite) there is a larger circulation pattern that influences the world's weather. This is known as the great ocean conveyor belt.

Water is somewhat like air: as it cools, it becomes denser and sinks. Salt also increases the density of water. Because it is so cold and salty, seawater off the coast of Greenland sinks to the deep ocean bottom and flows south to the South Atlantic. It then travels eastward along the Antarctic coastline and picks up more cold water from melting Antarctic ice. This deep, cold current then flows northward past New Zealand to the North Pacific, where it rises toward the surface and warms. Then the current flows southwest past northern Australia, across the Indian Ocean, around southern Africa, and north through the Atlantic to its starting point near Greenland. It may take more than 1,000 years for this great ocean conveyor belt to complete its circuit.

Because the conveyor belt is an important transporter of heat, it probably plays a key role in determining the global climate, and changes in the flow of the ocean conveyor belt may cause major climatic changes. Recent computer studies indicate that global warming (see page 140) may lead to rainfall increasing over the North Atlantic in the subsidence region of the conveyor belt. This would result in the seawater becoming less saline, slowing down the conveyor belt's circulation. The climate in western Europe would be most affected, and because the conveyor belt links all oceans, changes to the climate in other parts of the world are likely.

EL NIÑO AND LA NIÑA EVENTS

Occasionally in late December a warm current arrives off the western coast of South America near Ecuador and Peru. Scientists have termed this phenomenon El Niño, Spanish for *boy child*.

There is usually a bountiful harvest of anchovies in these cold, nutrient-rich ocean waters. However, with the arrival of an El Niño event the volume of anchovy catches suddenly plummets. An El Niño event also signals the beginning of heavy rainfall along the coastal deserts of Peru.

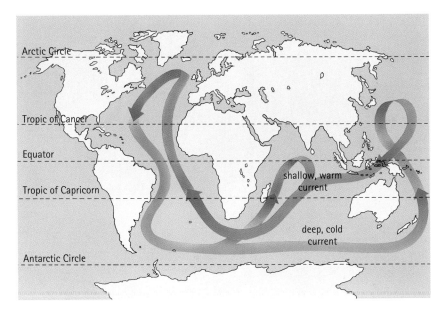

ABOVE: The great ocean conveyor belt is a system of deep, cold currents and shallow, warm currents that circles the globe.

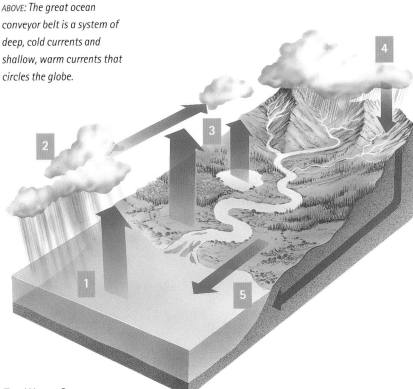

THE WATER CYCLE

1 Water from the ocean surface evaporates into the atmosphere.

2 The moist air forms clouds over the ocean. Some rain falls back into the ocean.

3 Moist air blows over land. Water evaporates from lakes, rivers, and the ground, and plant leaves give off moisture.

4 Precipitation falls over land and either supplements the water in rivers and streams or is absorbed by the ground.

5 Water returns to the oceans via rivers or underground seepage. The water cycle is completed.

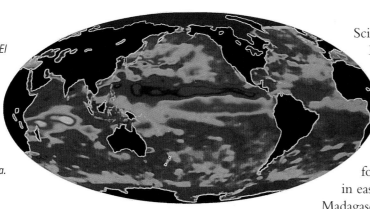

RIGHT: *This computer-enhanced map shows an El Niño event in November 1994. Warm water, represented by the orange-red area, has massed off the coasts of Colombia and Ecuador, in South America.*

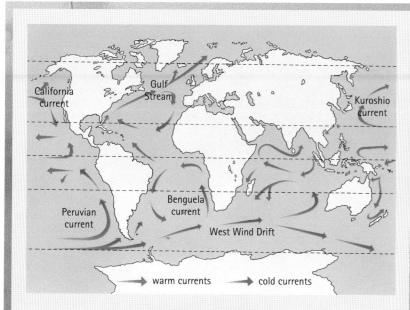

warm currents → cold currents

OCEAN CURRENTS

Oceans are highly efficient storers of heat. They transport warm or cool water around the earth and have a great influence on the climate of landmasses. For example, the warming effects of the Gulf Stream greatly moderate the climate of western Europe, which would otherwise be much more severe.

Ocean currents are mainly caused by the prevailing winds. The winds from the high-pressure systems in the mid-latitudes (see page 22) drive ocean currents that circulate in a clockwise direction in the Northern Hemisphere and counterclockwise in the south. Water temperatures are generally warmest near the Equator and coldest near the Poles. The highs produce cold currents on the western coasts of the continents and warm currents on the eastern coasts.

The major cold ocean currents, such as the Peruvian current and the Benguela current, tend to reduce rainfall over nearby land: the cool air above the current holds little moisture, so rain clouds are unlikely to form. The major warm currents, such as the Gulf Stream and the Kuroshio current, have the opposite effect: they produce warmer temperatures over nearby land. Large changes in sea-surface temperatures to the west of these currents favor the development of low-pressure centers, which results in heavy rain and strong winds over nearby land.

Scientists are still studying the cause of El Niño events. One theory under investigation proposes that a burst of strong, westerly winds from the West Pacific region transports a wave of warm water along the Equator to the east.

The consequences of El Niño events for global weather range from droughts in eastern Australia, northeast Brazil, Madagascar, Mozambique, and eastern parts of South Africa, to unusually wet weather in parts of Argentina, Uruguay, southern Brazil, and the southern United States. Climatic changes such as these indicate that changes in the atmospheric circulation occur with an El Niño event.

In 1924 Sir Gilbert Walker, then director-general of British observatories in India, identified a tendency for air pressure over the Pacific Ocean region to increase at the same time as air pressure over the Indian Ocean region decreases. Walker called this connection a southern oscillation.

In recent times scientists have made links between El Niño events and pressure patterns around the globe. One of these links is called the Southern Oscillation Index (SOI). The SOI is based on air-pressure differences between Tahiti, in the South Pacific, and Darwin, in northern Australia. When the air pressure over Darwin is higher than that over Tahiti, the SOI has a negative value. If this higher pressure persists over an extended period, the negative SOI is associated with an El Niño event.

If the reverse situation occurs, and the SOI is strongly positive for an extended period, scientists say that a La Niña event is taking place. A strong La Niña, which is Spanish for *girl child*, produces wet weather over Indonesia and eastern Australia, and dry conditions over the eastern South Pacific.

El Niño events tend to occur every three to eight years. Negative SOIs start about April and last for 12 months, but in the early 1990s an El Niño event lasted for three years. Scientists have recently suggested that this event was linked with climate changes caused by the enhanced greenhouse effect (see page 140).

THE DAILY WEATHER

THE WEATHER WE EXPERIENCE EVERY DAY
CAN RANGE FROM BLUE SKIES AND WHITE
CLOUDS TO THE TREMENDOUS FORCE OF A
THUNDERSTORM, AND FROM THICK FOG TO
THE GLORIOUS COLORS OF A RAINBOW
ARCHING ACROSS THE SKY. SOME
PHENOMENA, SUCH AS AURORAS, ARE LIMITED
IN EXTENT, WHILE OTHERS, SUCH AS WINDS,
OCCUR ALL OVER THE WORLD.

HOW CLOUDS FORM

The air we breathe is comprised mostly of nitrogen and oxygen. It also contains small amounts of other gases, including water vapor, which is water in an invisible, gaseous form.

CLOUDY WEATHER

As air cools it can hold less and less water vapor. Eventually, if air is cooled to a certain temperature, called the dewpoint, the water vapor changes into water droplets, a process known as condensation. The relative humidity of air (see page 20) when it's at its dewpoint is 100 percent—that is, the air is saturated with water vapor.

Clouds form when air rises, cools, and becomes saturated, at which point the water vapor condenses on minute particles and specks of dust in the atmosphere. These are called condensation nuclei, and billions of the tiny water droplets that have condensed on the nuclei together make a cloud. If the temperature of the air is below freezing point (32°F/0°C), the cloud may contain billions of tiny ice crystals as well as water droplets.

Because of their extremely small size these cloud droplets or crystals stay suspended in mid-air. In fact, they are so small that it takes one million of them to make a raindrop $1/12$ inch (2 mm) in diameter.

COOLING AIR

Normally, temperature decreases with height in the troposphere (see page 10). If air is made to rise, its temperature falls, and as it reaches saturation, condensation begins and clouds form. There are four main ways by which air is made to rise and cool as it moves across the earth's surface.

One of these ways is by the process of convection (see page 12). When the sun heats an area of ground, the air directly above it warms up. Because this mass of warm air is lighter than the surrounding air, it bubbles up into the sky (see illustration below left).

The second way air is lifted is by being forced up as it travels over hills, ridges, and mountains. This process is called orographic lifting (see illustration below center).

ABOVE LEFT: Lenticular clouds form when air is lifted and shaped by mountain waves (see page 32). Because these clouds look similar to flying saucers, it's thought some people have mistaken them for UFOs!

ABOVE: This bank of cloud has probably been formed by convection as well as by orographic lifting, thanks to the mountain range in the background.

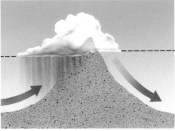
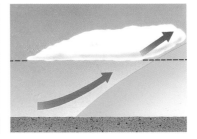

HOW CLOUDS FORM
Convection, far left, orographic lifting, center, and frontal systems, right, are three of the main ways in which air is lifted to form cloud. In each case the dotted line represents the condensation level, where water vapor condenses onto minute particles and specks in the atmosphere.

ABOVE: *The colors of these stormy-looking clouds over the Serengeti Plain in Tanzania form an eye-catching contrast to the golden hues of the grasslands below. The hot and flattish terrain produces convective clouds across extensive areas when there's sufficient moisture in the atmosphere.*

The third way air is lifted is by the action of warm and cold fronts (see page 26). Advancing cold air, known as a cold front, acts as a wedge that lifts warmer air in its path. Similarly, if advancing warm air, known as a warm front, meets denser, colder air in its path, the warmer air, being lighter, rises over the colder air mass (see illustration opposite right).

The fourth way air is lifted is by convergence as it approaches a low-pressure center (see page 28) and being forced to rise. This convergence of air results in widespread cloud cover and very often rain or snow, too.

TOWERING HEIGHTS

Once a cloud has formed, it may remain as a relatively shallow cloud or it may grow to a great height. A cloud will continue to grow as long as the rising air parcel remains warmer and lighter (more buoyant) than the surrounding air. When this occurs, conditions are said to be unstable and the cloud will keep bubbling up and up. Water vapor releases heat, called latent heat, when it condenses, and this makes lifted air even more unstable and buoyant. When the air is very unstable, the cloud may reach the top of the troposphere before it flattens out.

WHAT CLOUD IS THAT?

Clouds come in many shapes and sizes, from fluffy, white "pillows" floating just above the horizon, to wispy patches high in the sky, to formidable gray masses towering over the landscape—to mention just a few.

CLOUDS BY SHAPE AND HEIGHT

Although clouds display only a few basic forms, there are many combinations of these forms. English scientist Luke Howard (1772–1864) was the first person to name the clouds. In 1803 he used Latin words to distinguish three main cloud shapes: cumulus, stratus, and cirrus. *Cumulus*, meaning heap, describes the low-level, lumpy clouds that look rather like cauliflowers or pillows. *Stratus*, meaning layer, describes banks of sheetlike clouds. *Cirrus*, meaning tuft of hair, describes the high-level clouds that look wispy or threadlike.

Besides grouping them by shape, meteorologists classify clouds according to their altitude. In 1802 French naturalist Jean-Baptiste Lamarck (1744–1829) first proposed dividing the atmosphere into three regions. According to Lamarck's system, low-level clouds occur from sea level to 6,500 feet (1,950 m); mid-level clouds occur from 6,500 to 16,500 feet (1,950 to 4,950 m); and high-level clouds occur above 16,500 feet (4,950 m).

ABOVE: Cirrostratus clouds are tinged gold by the sun behind Barne Glacier, in the Antarctic.

RIGHT: Cumulus clouds cruise over the gorse-covered Cheviot Hills, in Northumberland, England. INSET: This wind-swept sky over Unst, in the Shetland Isles, Scotland, is filled with cirrus uncinus clouds.

LEFT: CLOUD CHART
Clouds are classified according to their shape and the height at which they form in the atmosphere. Most cumulonimbus clouds grow to reach the top of the troposphere.

Today, meteorologists across the world observe and describe clouds using a combination of Howard's and Lamarck's systems.

CLOUDS OF ALL KINDS

Cirrus clouds (or those whose name starts with cirro-) are high-level clouds. Thin, threadlike clouds, they sometimes become comma-shaped when they're twisted by the wind. Or they may appear as a thin, smooth veil (cirrostratus) or a regular pattern of small, lumpy clouds (cirrocumulus) covering all or part of the sky. Cirrus clouds are made up of ice crystals, and they sometimes herald an imminent change in the weather, such as rain, especially if they thicken and descend.

Mid-level clouds usually have a name that begins with alto-, such as altocumulus and altostratus. Altocumulus clouds often appear similar to cirrocumulus clouds, but their "lumps" are up to five times as large. One form of altocumulus cloud that is of special interest to weather forecasters is altocumulus castellanus. These turret-shaped clouds are signs of instability in the atmosphere and often presage the onset of thundery weather. Altostratus clouds are similar to cirrostratus clouds, but they are lower and are often thick enough to block out the sun.

Low-level clouds are stratus (smooth sheets), stratocumulus (rolls of cloud that often have merged), and cumulus (heaped clouds). A cumulus cloud may have its growth capped by a layer of warmer air higher up. In this case it's called a fair-weather cumulus because it can't grow any more and is unlikely to produce rain. But if the conditions are right (see page 40), cumulus clouds may grow to great heights or thicken and darken to become cumulonimbus (thunder clouds).

Even though cumulonimbus clouds start growing at a low level, they can extend high into the troposphere. The tropopause acts as a lid to their growth, causing them to spread out horizontally (see page 10). When a cumulo-nimbus cloud grows very tall, it contains a large quantity of ice crystals and can produce damaging hail, destructive winds, flooding rains, and tornadoes (see pages 47, 48, and 62).

CLOUD TERMINOLOGY

In the scientific community Latin terms are internationally understood. Meteorologists use various Latin terms to describe clouds. Some of the most common cloud terms are:

castellanus	turret-shaped
congestus	swollen, developing
fibratus	forming in strands
humilis	humble, small
lenticularis	lens-shaped
mediocris	average, medium-sized
nimbus	rain-bearing
uncinus	hooked
undulatus	forming in waves

BLOW, WINDS, BLOW

LEFT: *These trees growing near the coast in Brittany, France, have been bent by the wind. In this region the winds are prevailing westerlies, which often blow strongly during the winter months.*

RIGHT: *Sandstone formations on the Colorado Plateau, in the United States, have been weathered into intricate shapes. There is little vegetation to block wind and anchor the soil in arid areas such as these, so large areas are exposed to the wind and are subject to erosion.*

In addition to the major global winds, local winds are a significant aspect of the weather. These winds result when local temperature contrasts or physical barriers, such as mountain ranges, affect the flow of wind.

SEA AND LAND BREEZES

The most familiar local winds caused by temperature contrasts are sea breezes. Although both land and sea receive the same amount of solar radiation during the day, the land's surface heats up more quickly than the sea. The air over land rises as it's heated, producing an area of low pressure, and cooler air from over the ocean rushes in to replace it. The warmer air cools as it rises and moves out over the ocean before sinking again, creating a circulation of air (see illustration below left).

Land breezes are the reverse of sea breezes. At night the land cools down more quickly than the sea surface, and the warmer air over the ocean rises. The cooler air over the land moves in to replace it. The warmer ocean air cools as it rises, before moving toward the land and sinking again, creating a reverse circulation of air (see illustration far right). The temper-

ature contrast between land and sea is not as marked at night as it is during the day, so land breezes are not usually as strong as sea breezes.

VALLEY AND MOUNTAIN WINDS

Other significant local winds caused by temperature contrasts are valley and mountain winds. Valley, or anabatic, winds form when the sun heats valley slopes and warmed air over the slopes rises. The air over the slopes has a lower pressure than the air at the same level over the valley, which leads to the formation of a valley breeze toward and up the slopes (see illustration opposite left). Aloft, the rising air on the slopes cools and moves away from the slopes to create a circulation of air. The breeze will continue as long as the sun heats the slopes.

SEA AND LAND BREEZES

Sea breezes, below left, form when colder air from over the ocean rushes in to replace warmer air rising over land. The reverse process occurs at night, below, when cooler air over land moves over the ocean to replace warmer air, forming a land breeze.

VALLEY AND MOUNTAIN WINDS

During the day the sun warms air over valley slopes, below. The air rises, creating a valley, or anabatic, wind. At night air over the slopes cools and sinks to the valley floor, below right, forming a mountain, or katabatic, wind.

Mountain, or katabatic, winds are the reverse of valley winds. They form at night when air close to the slope becomes colder and heavier than air at the same level farther away from the slope. Gravity causes the heavier air to drain down the slope. This air is replaced by air from the free atmosphere high above the valley floor drifting onto the slopes, where it, too, is cooled and drawn by gravity down into the valley (see illustration below right). If the

cool air drains gently to an open valley floor, it often forms mist, fog, or frost. But if the air drains quite strongly, particularly if it's funneled through a narrow valley, high-speed mountain winds can form.

The bora (a cold wind from the Dinaric Alps, in Croatia) often exceeds 35 miles per hour (55 km/h), with gusts up to 60 miles per hour (100 km/h). The mistral, a cold, dry wind funneled through France's Rhône Valley, reaches similar speeds.

A famous local wind caused when a mountain range obstructs wind flow is the foehn, a warm, dry wind on the leeward side of mountains. The term originally referred to warm winds in the Swiss Alps, but is now used to refer to any winds caused by the foehn process—for example, the chinook of the Rocky Mountains, in North America.

RAIN, HAIL, AND SHOWERS

Rain is one of the main ways water in the atmosphere returns to the oceans, an important part of the water cycle (see page 34). Rain is also vital for replenishing the earth's freshwater supplies, which make up only 3 percent of the water on the planet.

RAINY DAYS

Rain, as opposed to showers, falls from layered, or stratiform, clouds (see page 42). These may extend for thousands of square miles, and once the rain sets in, it probably won't stop for some time. A shower, on the other hand, is rainfall from a cumuliform cloud, which may extend only 10 square miles (26 sq. km) or less. The shower starts and finishes abruptly and can quickly give way to sunshine.

Precipitation (rain, snow, or hail) forms when there is a build-up of cloud droplets or ice crystals in a cloud. There are two main ways for precipitation to form: coalescence and the ice-crystal process.

In clouds where the air temperature is above freezing (more than 32°F/0°C), coalescence occurs. The minute water droplets in clouds are usually so tiny that they remain suspended in mid-air. However, updrafts in the cloud enhance the collision of the droplets. As they collide, the bigger droplets gather up the smaller ones and grow even larger. Eventually, these droplets become heavy enough to fall to the ground as raindrops.

Precipitation forms by the ice-crystal process when cloud made up of supercooled water droplets and ice crystals exists above the freezing level. Supercooled droplets consist of water that is below freezing point but has not frozen. Water vapor diffuses from the super-cooled droplets to the ice crystals, causing the crystals to grow.

Droplets can exist in this supercooled state until they reach temperatures as low as minus 40°F (−40°C), when nearly all the droplets will be frozen. Most, however, freeze well before this extreme cold is reached.

The process by which water vapor changes directly into ice without first condensing, or becoming liquid, is known as sublimation. Water vapor in very cold cloud sublimates when there are suitable particles, such as ice crystals, on which it can freeze.

Once the crystals become large enough, they start to fall to the ground. They grow further in their fall by colliding and coalescing with other crystals or with water droplets.

RAIN OR DRIZZLE

Meteorologists classify precipitation according to the form and size of the drops or crystals when they reach the ground. Once ice crystals fall from a cloud, for instance, they either melt or remain frozen, depending on the tempera-

LEFT: Heavy rain has flooded parts of this freeway in Germany, causing cars to aquaplane along the road. Intense rainfall over urban environments can lead to flash flooding. This is because extensive areas of bitumen and concrete absorb little water, and create a large volume of runoff.

TYPES OF PRECIPITATION
The type of precipitation that falls depends on the process that formed it and the temperature of the air below the cloud. Above the freezing level the main way precipitation forms is the ice-crystal process; below the freezing level coalescence becomes more important. At the base of the illustration the red panels represent air that has a temperature above freezing, and the blue panels represent air that is below freezing.

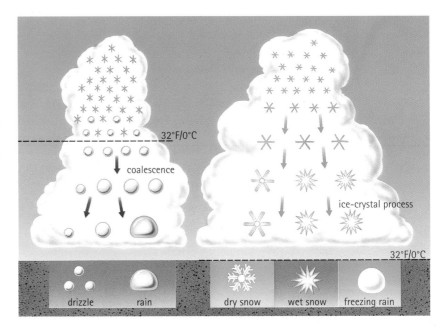

ture of the air below the cloud. If they melt, they become rain or wet snow; if they remain frozen, they fall as dry snow (see page 54).

Meteorologists classify liquid water drops as drizzle when the drop size is at least $\frac{1}{125}$ inch (0.2 mm), and as rain when the drop size is more than $\frac{1}{50}$ inch (0.5 mm).

Freezing rain forms when supercooled water drops in the cloud fall as rain and turn to ice when they meet colder air (forming ice pellets), or meet a surface where the temperature is near or below freezing point (forming glaze).

FALLING BALLS OF ICE: HAIL

In thunderstorm clouds (see page 48) ice crystals falling toward the ground can get caught in strong updrafts and be carried aloft many times over. This causes them to grow rapidly, and they reach the ground as balls of ice, or hailstones. The diameter of these hailstones can be $\frac{1}{5}$ to 2 inches (5 to 50 mm), or even more. Falling hailstones that have a diameter of 1 inch (25 mm) or more can damage cars and windows and sting painfully when they fall on people.

BELOW: A spring shower sprinkles a lone linden tree. Linden trees don't tolerate drought well; they grow in temperate zones in the Northern Hemisphere, where rainfall is fairly constant throughout the year.

THOR SPEAKS: THUNDERSTORMS

According to Norse mythology, Thor was the god of thunder and lightning (see page 117), and he was held responsible for some powerful weather indeed. There are more than 40,000 thunderstorms around the world every day, and the largest of these storms possess the energy of a nuclear bomb.

A STORM BREWS

Thunderstorms can be an awesome sight: huge cumulonimbus clouds swell higher and higher into the atmosphere, accompanied by lightning streaking across a dark gray or purple sky. Thunder may rumble in the distance or crack like a whip overhead. Such storms can also generate destructive weather such as hail and tornadoes (see pages 17 and 62).

ABOVE: *A cumulonimbus cloud with an anvil top and cloud-to-ground lightning looms over Darwin, in tropical northern Australia. Tropical regions experience many more thunderstorms than places at higher latitudes.*

LIFECYCLE OF A THUNDERSTORM

1 In the first stage of a thunderstorm a cumulus cloud begins to grow. Vigorous updrafts develop, which prevent any precipitation falling.

2 In the mature stage downdrafts also develop, and showers or hail may fall. Lightning and thunder and squally surface winds may occur.

3 During the final stage the downdrafts cut off the supply of warm updrafts, and the cloud begins to collapse. Precipitation ceases. Altocumulus and cirrus clouds may form above the shrinking cumulus cloud.

Thunderstorms have a lifecycle with distinct stages. For a thunderstorm to form, there must be atmospheric instability (see page 41), accompanied by moist air that has been lifted. Provided the atmosphere remains unstable, the air will continue to rise and create a giant cumulus congestus cloud (see page 85) with the top growing at 16 to 32 feet (5 to 10 m) per second. During the first stage of the thunderstorm, which lasts 10 to 15 minutes, there are warm updrafts throughout the cloud.

The second, or mature, stage lasts for 15 to 30 minutes. The cloud has grown to become a towering cumulonimbus (see page 86), and the top is so high that it is composed mostly of ice crystals. The high-altitude winds blow the top of the cloud out so it resembles a giant anvil in the sky. Cold, fast-moving downdrafts develop. These are created by air that has been chilled high in the cloud, and their speed is enhanced by the pull of falling water droplets or ice particles. The thunderstorm produces rain, snow, or hail.

Thunder and lightning occur during the second stage. The collision of water droplets and ice crystals inside the cloud produces opposing electrical charges. The discharge of electricity creates lightning (see page 50). The lightning stroke rapidly heats the air, which expands and sends out a shockwave. We hear this as thunder.

ABOVE: *A truck in the Southwest United States races along the road ahead of an approaching squall line. Squall lines often extend for hundreds of miles and can last several hours.*

In the third, or dissipating, stage the downdrafts spread throughout the cloud and eventually cut off the supply of moist updrafts needed to maintain the thunderstorm. The precipitation soon ceases and cloud droplets gradually evaporate. This final stage may last for up to an hour.

BELOW: A well-developed squall line has formed on the base of a severe thunderstorm in Darwin, Australia.

MULTICELLS, SUPERCELLS, AND SQUALL LINES

Multicell thunderstorms consist of several cells, or individual storms, in clusters at various stages of development. Multicell storms are self-propagating because their cold downdrafts spread out when they reach the surface and lift warmer, moist air to form new cells.

Many thunderstorms produce severe weather and leave a trail of damage in their wake, but the king of damaging thunderstorms is the supercell. Supercells can produce very heavy rain, large hailstones, destructive winds, and tornadoes. Because of changes in the direction and speed of winds aloft, the updrafts in supercells are tilted. They rise over the cold downdrafts, enabling these storms to last for some hours because their supply of moist updrafts isn't cut off by the downdrafts.

Thunderstorms are sometimes arranged along a line of low pressure. This is known as a squall line, because the downdrafts cause gusty winds at the surface. A fully formed squall line is constantly regenerated by the cooler downdrafts, which lift warmer, moist air in its path.

ELECTRIC SKIES: LIGHTNING

Inky black and purple skies rent by sparking bolts of electricity; towering cumulonimbus clouds piled high in the troposphere; a sudden, loud crack of thunder—the sight and sound of lightning can be a truly dramatic experience.

ELECTRICAL DISCHARGES

Lightning is simply a sudden flash of light caused by an electrical discharge—nothing more than a spark really, but a very big one. It may occur within a cloud, between cloud and ground, between a cloud and nearby air, or between clouds.

Electrical charges build up in cumulonimbus clouds. Scientists are not entirely sure why these charges develop, but some believe they are the result of rising cloud droplets and ice crystals colliding with heavier, falling particles, such as hailstones.

Positive and negative charges are attracted to one another. When electrically charged particles of opposite sign move toward one another, an electrical discharge occurs that causes a spark, which we see as lightning.

In a cumulonimbus cloud positive charges form in the top of the cloud, negative charges form in the central and lower parts, and a small positive charge forms near the cloud base.

This net negative charge in the lower part of the thunderstorm cloud induces a positive charge on the ground below. Up to a point air will insulate the charges from each other, keeping them apart. But the difference between the charges can build to such an extent that the air can no longer insulate them. Then the negatively charged particles in the cloud begin to search out the path of least resistance to ground. This is the beginning of a lightning stroke, called a stepped leader.

The stepped leader advances in a series of steps of 165 feet (50 m) or so at a time, pausing about 50 millionths of a second between each one. When it's close to the ground, a return stroke travels up from the ground to meet it. Once the circuit is closed, there is a flood of negative charges from cloud to ground, and a return flow of positive charge from ground to cloud, which creates a highly luminous flash—the lightning stroke.

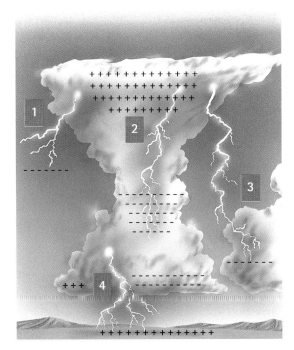

TYPES OF LIGHTNING

The different types of lightning that can occur depend on the location of opposing electrical charges both within and around the cloud.

1. Cloud-to-air lightning.
2. Lightning within the cloud.
3. Cloud-to-cloud lightning.
4. Cloud-to-ground lightning.

The lightning stroke discharges about 100 million volts of electricity, and the temperature of the air along the lightning path is suddenly heated to 54,000°F (30,000°C). This causes air pressure in the lightning path to rise, and the air rapidly expands. The expansion of air creates a shock wave that we hear as thunder.

DIFFERENT TYPES OF LIGHTNING

Lightning often appears with many branches along the main channel. This is called streak, or forked, lightning. The branching is due to electrical discharges to the electrical field that is naturally present in the atmosphere. If the lightning takes a particularly tortuous path between cloud and ground, it's known as ribbon lightning.

The electrical discharge may also occur between the positive and negative charge centers within the cloud, or between charge centers of opposite sign in adjacent clouds. From the ground we see this lightning as a dispersed flash because it's obscured by cloud. It's known as sheet lightning.

A somewhat rare form of lightning is pearl-necklace lightning, also known as chain or bead lightning. The brightness along the lightning path varies, and this gives the stroke the appearance of pearls on a string.

RIGHT AND INSET: A summer thunderstorm over Tucson, Arizona, fires off a double volley of forked cloud-to-ground lightning across the night sky.

CALCULATING THE DISTANCE OF LIGHTNING

We hear thunder either as a loud crack if the lightning's close by, or as a low, rumbling sound if it's more distant. Because light travels at 186,282 miles per second (299,792 km/s), we see the lightning flash almost as soon as it occurs. But because sound takes 5 seconds to travel 1 mile (3 seconds/km), it's often many seconds before we hear thunder.

To estimate how far away the lightning is, count the number of seconds between seeing the lightning and hearing the thunder. Then divide the number of seconds by 5 to calculate the distance of the lightning in miles (or by 3 for km). Usually, the sound of thunder isn't audible more than 15 miles (25 km) from a lightning discharge.

FOG, MIST, AND DEW

White mist floating over a glassy lake, dew-covered grass glinting in the sun, deep valleys filled with thick fog—all are examples of water in the atmosphere that has condensed. When air is cooled to a certain temperature, called its dewpoint, it can hold no more water vapor, and is said to be saturated. At the dewpoint the vapor will start to become liquid, or condense, and masses of tiny water droplets either become suspended in mid-air as cloud or fog, or settle on the ground as dew.

MISTY MORNINGS, FOGGY NIGHTS

If water vapor in air above the ground condenses, clouds form (see page 40). If water vapor in air in contact with the ground condenses, mist or fog forms. With both types of weather, there have to be atmospheric particles, such as dust specks, for water vapor to condense on. Such particles are always present in the air.

Mist is a light fog. Meteorologists define fog as conditions where visibility is restricted to less than 3,280 feet (1 km). They define mist as conditions where visibility is restricted but greater than 3,280 feet (1 km).

There are three main types of fog: radiation, advection, and upslope fog (see pages 80–1). Radiation fog forms on cool, clear, calm nights, when the earth's surface and the air in contact with it both cool. The cooled surface air gently mixes with and cools the air above it. If the air continues to cool until it reaches its dewpoint, a thin fog forms. The fog cools the air above it, and the depth of the fog increases.

In the morning the sun's rays warm the ground, especially near the edges of the fog. The air in contact with the ground becomes mildly turbulent as it is heated, mixes with the saturated, foggy air, and the fog gradually

shrinks and disappears. The last remnants of a bank of fog that shrinks upward in this way is known as fog stratus (see illustration below).

Advection fog can develop when warm, moist air travels over a cold surface. For instance, a type of advection fog called sea fog can develop when warm, moist air from over a warm current flows over cold water. Advection fog also occurs when warm, moist air from over the ocean flows over a cooler landmass (see illustration opposite).

Another type of fog, called steam fog, forms when cold air passes over warmer water. Water constantly evaporates from the surface of the ocean and other bodies of water. In relatively still conditions the cold air can quickly become saturated with the evaporating water. The water vapor condenses, and gentle convective currents carry the water droplets

TOP: *Mist floats over a frost-covered landscape near Berne, in Switzerland. Frost, mist, and dew may occur together, because the conditions needed for them to form are quite similar.*

ABOVE: *Daisies reflected in dew drops on a flower stalk.*

FOG STRATUS

As the sun rises, it warms the edges of a bank of fog that has formed during the night. The fog bank shrinks as the sun rises higher. By mid-morning a thin deck of fog stratus may remain suspended in mid-air.

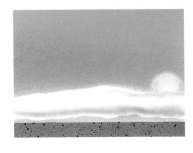

ABOVE: Advection fog has formed over a lake in Tasmania, Australia, and is being evaporated by the early morning sun.

upward into drier air. Here they evaporate, creating the appearance of steam or smoke rising from the water surface. If a layer of warmer air, known as an inversion, traps the moisture-laden cold air, water continues to evaporate, which saturates the air and forms fog. This fog is also known as arctic sea smoke.

Upslope fog forms when air is forced to rise gently up a slope, such as when light winds move over hilly terrain. The air cools as it

moves up the slope, until it reaches its dewpoint and fog forms. Frontal fogs occur along a front (see page 26) when rain falls from a warmer air mass into colder air. The raindrops evaporate and saturate the cooler surface air, and the water begins to condense again, forming fog.

DEWY DELIGHTS

Dew forms when water vapor condenses directly on the ground or some other surface, such as leaves or blades of grass. Dew usually forms on clear, still nights when a layer of air close to the ground is cooled. It usually disappears by mid-morning when the sun's heat evaporates it. If fog forms, dew is present, but dew is not always accompanied by fog.

If the temperature drops below freezing (32°F/0°C) after the dew has formed, the dew drops freeze and become hoar frost (see page 54).

ADVECTION FOG

When air above a warm ocean area is blown across a colder landmass, advection fog can form. This often produces large areas of coastal fog in Britain, because of the nearby warm waters of the Gulf Stream.

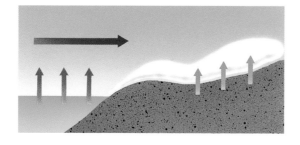

SNOW, SLEET, AND FROST

Snow, sleet, and frost all form when the air temperature is below freezing (32°F/0°C). Snow and sleet are forms of precipitation that fall from clouds; frost is the result of ice forming on the ground or other surfaces.

SNOWY CONDITIONS

Snow starts as minute ice crystals in cold clouds. These tiny crystals grow by the ice-crystal process (see pages 46–7) to form snowflakes, which fall to the ground when they become large enough.

If the air temperature below the cloud is below freezing, the snowflakes settle on the ground as dry snow. But if the temperature is above freezing, the snowflakes start to melt before they reach the ground and become either wet snow or rain.

Snowflakes vary greatly in size. At temperatures well below freezing, snow consists of very small ice crystals with a diameter usually less than ¹/₂₅ inch (1 mm). At temperatures near freezing point the ice crystals stick together, forming snowflakes that may be 2 to 3 inches (5 to 7.5 cm) across.

Ice crystals that make up snow take a variety of shapes, depending on the temperature of the cloud in which they form. At minus 20°F (–29°C) and below, the ice crystals form six-sided columns; from minus 10°F to 0°F

BELOW: *A snowstorm in New York City creates uncomfortable conditions for pedestrians. The city averages about 20 to 40 inches (50 to 100 cm) of snow a year.*

LEFT: This freezing rain on tree branches, known as glaze (see page 90), has been shaped and elongated by the wind.

RIGHT: Heavy frost mantles trees and shrubs in Argyll, Scotland. Overnight temperatures have to be very low for frost to extend to the tops of trees.

BELOW LEFT: An aerial view of the Rocky Mountains in the United States reveals extensive snow cover. Snow persists on the higher peaks even during summer.

BELOW RIGHT: Snow can occur even in desert regions, as this photograph of sand dunes in Utah shows. The only areas of the mainland United States that have never experienced snow, as far as the records are concerned, are southern Florida and the Florida Keys.

(−23°C to −18°C) they are flat, six-sided plates; from 0°F to 20°F (−18°C to −7°C) they are fernlike; and from 20°F to 32°F (−7°C to 0°C) they are needlelike.

Snow on the ground traps air beneath it and is an excellent insulator. In cold climates snow cover protects plants from extreme cold on long, winter nights. During the spring thaw snow melt is an important source of water for plants.

However, snow can be a hazard when heavy snowfalls are accompanied by strong winds. Such snowstorms can reduce visibility almost to zero and severely disrupt towns and cities. When falling or swirling snow reduces visibility to 500 feet (150 m) or less, winds are 35 miles per hour (56 km/h) or stronger, and temperatures are 10°F (−12°C) or below, meteorologists define the snowstorm as a blizzard.

SLEET AND FROST

Meteorologists use the term *sleet* to describe small pellets of ice up to ⅕ inch (5 mm) in diameter (see page 90). The pellets form when supercooled raindrops fall through a layer of air that is below freezing. The term is also used to describe a mixture of snow and rain. Snow melts if it falls through air temperatures above freezing. The surrounding air provides the heat required to melt the snow, and this heat loss can chill the air to below freezing. Some of the raindrops will then refreeze, and a mixture of snow and rain, or sleet, settles on the ground.

Frost, like dew (see page 53), forms on cold, still nights when the temperature falls below freezing. The most common type is hoar frost, which is a cover of feathery ice crystals that forms when dew freezes on the ground or other surfaces. It may also be a mixture of frozen dew and water vapor that has frozen without first becoming liquid. Less common is rime frost, a deposit of rough ice crystals that forms when supercooled water droplets (water that's below freezing point but remains liquid) in fog touch a surface below freezing and turn to ice.

COLORS IN THE SKY

When sunlight is bent or scattered in some way, a brilliant array of colors may be displayed. On a clear day the sky appears a brilliant blue, while it may glow a fiery orange-red at sunrise or sunset. Sometimes rainbows arch across the horizon, or bright, iridescent patches of color appear around the sun.

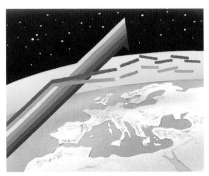

COLOR AND LIGHT

The sun continuously emits energy as electromagnetic radiation. Almost half this energy is visible to the human eye in the form of light. The sun also emits energy that we can't see, such as ultraviolet (UV) radiation, which may cause sunburn, and infrared radiation, which produces heat.

Although the light we see is white, it's actually made up of a spectrum of colors: red, orange, yellow, green, blue, indigo, and violet. When white light is bent or dispersed, such as when it passes through a prism (see illustration below), it breaks up into its constituent colors.

Light travels through space like a series of pulses, or waves. Each color has its own wavelength; that is, the distance between any one point on a pulse and the same point on the following pulse. Colors in the red end of the spectrum have the longest wavelengths; colors in the violet end have the shortest wavelengths.

RED AND BLUE SKIES

As light travels through the earth's atmosphere, air molecules scatter the rays in different directions. They scatter more of the short-wave blue colors than they do the long-wave red colors, so we see the sky as blue on clear days.

Because the sun is low on the horizon at sunrise or sunset, light travels farther through the atmosphere. Air molecules scatter the short-wave colors out of the beam, leaving the longer wavelengths, the orange and red rays, to reach us. This is why we see red or orange skies near the horizon at sunrise or sunset.

When sunlight enters raindrops, they act as tiny prisms, refracting the light. Inside the drops the colors are reflected, and then refracted again when they exit the drops. Each color emerges separately, forming a primary rainbow with red on top and violet on the bottom (see page 96

and illustration below). Sometimes the colors are reflected twice inside the raindrops. This forms a secondary bow 9° above the primary bow. In a secondary bow the colors are reversed; that is, violet is on top and red is on the bottom.

COLORS AROUND THE SUN AND MOON

A colored ring around the sun or moon, called a corona, forms when raindrops in altocumulus or altostratus clouds disperse, or diffract, the colors of white light (see page 96).

Sometimes tinted patches of red and green, or blue and yellow, are visible on clouds. Called iridescence, this is a partial corona caused by very small cloud droplets diffracting sunlight (see page 97).

Haloes are white or faintly colored circles of luminescence around the sun or moon. They form when ice crystals in cirrostratus clouds refract, or bend, light (see page 97).

Sundogs, or mock suns, are two bright spots either side of the sun. They are formed by the refraction of light by ice crystals, and are also known as parhelia (see page 98).

BLUE AND RED SKIES

As sunlight travels toward earth during the day, left, air molecules scatter the constituent colors. Blue rays are scattered more than the other colors, so we see the sky as blue. At sunrise and sunset, right, sunlight travels farther through the atmosphere and more short-wave colors are scattered out of the beam, leaving only the red and orange rays to reach us.

RIGHT: A rainbow arching across the sky forms a colorful backdrop at sunset in Denali National Park, Alaska. Rainbows form only when the sun is low on the horizon, such as early in the morning or late in the afternoon.

HOW A RAINBOW FORMS

For a rainbow to form, there need to be sunlight and rain at the same time. Raindrops act like tiny prisms, refracting the light when it enters the drop and again when it exits. Sunlight exits the raindrops at an angle of 42° relative to its original direction.

TOP: *An aurora borealis illuminates the sky. Auroras form when charged particles from the sun collide with gas molecules in the atmosphere (see page 98).*

CENTER: *The color of this crimson-red sky is enhanced by smoke particles in the atmosphere, which scatter short-wave colors out of the beam, while allowing red and orange rays through.*

BOTTOM: *A halo encircles the sun, and cirrostratus clouds streak across the sky.*

THE POWER OF WEATHER

EVERY DAY, AND IN DIFFERENT WAYS, WEATHER INFLUENCES OUR LIVES. FROM HURRICANES TO TORNADOES, WILDFIRES TO MONSOON FLOODS, WEATHER REVEALS ITS MIGHT ALL OVER THE WORLD. OUR ABILITY TO TAP THE ENERGY CONTAINED IN SUNLIGHT, WIND, RAIN, AND OCEAN WATER WILL INFLUENCE THE SHAPE OF FUTURE TECHNOLOGIES.

TWISTERS: DUST DEVILS AND WATERSPOUTS

The term *twisters* is used to describe a wide range of localized, tightly rotating winds. Some are harmless, lasting only a few seconds, while others may persist an hour or more. But some twisters are so devastating, they last a lifetime—in people's memories.

WHIRLWINDS AND DEVILISH DUST

On a windy day anywhere in the world it's likely that a number of short-lived whirlwinds will spin their way across the landscape. They are visible from what they pick up from the ground, be it dust, snow, or litter. Usually, these very weak common twisters are simply eddies in the wind as it blows past buildings, trees, or other obstacles, and are similar to the eddies in a river as it flows past large rocks.

Another form of twister, the dust devil, is quite common in warm rural areas, more so in dry desert regions. Unlike waterspouts and tornadoes (see page 62), these twisters are not attached to clouds. As the sun heats the ground, currents of warm air, known as thermals, rise in localized areas. Thermals tend to be stronger over certain terrain, such as small hills. Slight variations in the wind speed and direction just above the ground can cause these thermals to intensify, drawing in air from near the surface, which spirals upwards. Any loose dust or sand will be drawn into the spiral, giving it a dusty appearance—hence the name *dust devil*.

These twisters tend to last only a few minutes. Usually they are a few feet across and no more than about 330 feet (100 m) high; the most intense devils are seldom higher than 3,300 feet (1,000 m). The wind speed inside these twisters peaks at about 55 miles per hour (90 km/h), making them more of a nuisance than a real danger, but they have been known to cause light aircraft to flip over during takeoff or landing.

WATERY FUNNELS

Waterspouts are quite common over warm oceans and lakes and are sometimes found in temperate regions. A delicate funnel reaches from the base of a towering cumulus cloud down to the water, where it kicks up a skirt of spray. Waterspouts are most likely to occur when large cumulus clouds form over water, and the wind varies in its speed and direction near the water surface. The variations in wind cause updrafts of warm air to start rotating early in the cloud's development. These updrafts strengthen as the cloud grows, causing the waterspout to intensify. Some water is sucked up by the funnel, but much of the funnel's color and shape is formed when moisture condenses as the air rises and cools.

Waterspouts can vary dramatically in intensity but generally remain quite weak. The base may vary from a few feet to about 330 feet (100 m) across. Most generate peak winds of less than 60 miles per hour (100 km/h), but one estimate from film footage indicated wind speeds up to 190 miles per hour (305 km/h). Regardless of their speed, they pose a hazard to small craft such as power boats and yachts.

Sometimes a fully developed tornado (a twister that forms over land) will move over water and draw water up into its parent cloud. This is called a tornadic waterspout to distinguish it from its weaker relatives, which are called simply waterspouts.

Tornadic waterspouts may suck up large quantities of water, and tales of frogs and fish raining down have been attributed to these stronger waterspouts. It's possible for them to suck up unfortunate creatures such as frogs or fish out of shallow lakes, only to let them fall to the ground some distance away.

ABOVE: *Here a waterspout has formed a perfectly vertical funnel, which dangles from the base of a cumulus cloud.*

RIGHT: *A dust devil in Central Australia. In this part of the world dust devils are known as willy-willies. They are sometimes strong enough to damage buildings.*

LEFT: *A dust devil on the slopes of Gelungung volcano, in Java, Indonesia. The funnel's light gray color is due to the fine, volcanic ash it is drawing in.*

TWISTERS: TORNADOES

Tornadoes, often wrongly referred to as minicyclones, are the most violent of nature's wind storms. A tornado's funnel, or vortex, extends from the base of a cumulonimbus cloud to the ground. It's a whirling mass of air with very low pressure at its center that sucks up almost anything in its path.

TORNADO ALLEY

Tornadoes have been reported on every continent in the world, except Antarctica. A research group estimated that almost 500 tornadoes affected the United States in May 1996. Kansas, Missouri, and Oklahoma have by far the greatest number of tornadoes, which are as severe as any in the world, and this region has been nicknamed Tornado Alley.

Most tornadoes last only a few minutes and have a damage path of no more than 165 feet (50 m) wide and 3 miles (5 km) long, so they usually bring devastation to a narrow swath of land. But the most severe tornadoes can be up to 1 mile (1.6 km) across, last an hour, and have damage paths as long as 60 miles (100 km).

RIGHT: *The funnel, or vortex, of this Nevada tornado can be clearly seen. Tornadic winds tend to blow counter-clockwise in the Northern Hemisphere and clockwise in the Southern Hemisphere, although there have been some exceptions.*

TACKLING TWISTERS

Because tornadoes whip up winds so powerful that they would destroy normal wind-measuring instruments, there are few reliable measurements of peak wind speeds. Researchers are now using portable Doppler radar (see page 124) to measure wind speed, so they can stand well away from the action! In 1991 a researcher using Doppler radar in the United States measured wind speeds of up to 280 miles per hour (450 km/h) in one tornado.

Because measuring winds in tornadoes was so difficult, Japanese-born researcher T. Theodore Fujita devised an intensity scale based on the damage done to buildings and trees: F0 light damage; F1 moderate damage; F2 considerable damage; F3 severe damage; F4 devastating damage; F5 incredible damage.

TORNADO FORMING: WARNING! WARNING!

Tornadoes tend to occur with the most severe, longer lived thunderstorms, known as super-cells (see page 49), and are also relatively common with thunderstorms in the feeder bands of hurricanes (see page 66).

Recent investigations have shown that tornadoes may form in different ways. If winds outside a thunderstorm blow in different directions and speeds at various heights, they can cause updrafts of air feeding into the thunderstorm base to start rotating. Often this air rotating strongly in the middle of the storm, called the mesocyclone, is the first sign that a tornado is forming. Next the funnel descends from the center of the mesocyclone until it touches the ground.

With radar, forecasters can detect a meso-cyclone forming up to 20 minutes before the funnel touches down and issue advance warnings. But not every mesocyclone produces a tornado, and many tornadoes may not be detected by radar.

In the 1990s a research experiment in the United States found that in many storms the funnel forms at the same time as the meso-cyclone. Although radar can pick up the mesocyclone, there's no advance warning that the funnel's about to touch down. So by the time the radar detects the mesocyclone, the tornado's already on the ground causing havoc!

LEFT: The sight of a tornado approaching can be terrifying. The National Weather Service uses a network of Doppler radar across the continental United States to provide a tornado-warning service.

FORMATION OF A TORNADO

1 Varying wind speed and direction cause the updraft to rotate.

2 The spiraling updraft of air feeds the storm.

3 Cold downdrafts from the upper levels of the cloud reach the ground.

4 The inflow of warm air at the base of the cloud also spirals upward.

5 A spinning column of air, the funnel, forms at the cloud base.

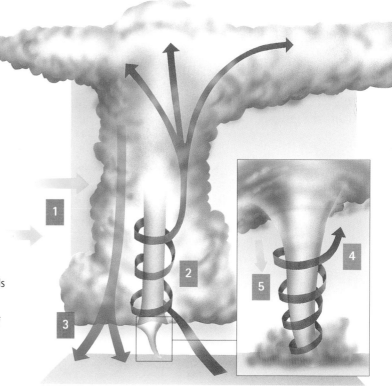

MICROBURSTS, DUST STORMS, AND WILDFIRES

The recent history of the United States could well have been different had a certain flight into Andrews Air Force Base arrived a few minutes later. On August 1, 1983, Air Force One—with President Ronald Reagan on board—landed at Andrews base only six minutes before the strongest microburst ever recorded. The wind changed from a 150-mile-per-hour (240 km/h) head wind to a 97-mile-per-hour (156 km/h) tail wind, a phenomenon known as wind shear.

SHEAR WINDS

For an aircraft landing or taking off, such a change in airspeed can be catastrophic, causing the airplane to either under- or overshoot the runway and possibly crash.

A microburst is a short-lived but intense wind squall that radiates from a central point. It typically starts some 3 miles (5 km) above the ground, usually inside a towering cumulus or cumulonimbus cloud. Precipitation starts to fall inside the cloud, dragging the nearby air down with it. The descending air evaporates and becomes colder and heavier than the surrounding air. Below the cloud base, precipitation in the downdraft evaporates further, making the air even colder. The cold air accelerates downward until it hits the ground. Here it forms a circular vortex that rapidly spreads away from its touchdown point, bringing a burst of very strong winds—the microburst.

If there is still rain in the downdraft when it touches the ground, it is known as a wet microburst. If the air below the cloud base is relatively dry, all the rain may evaporate in mid-air to form a dry microburst. Dry microbursts are often visible only from the dust and debris they pick up, but the evaporating rain may be seen as a dark fringe, known as virga, hanging from the cloud.

WALLS OF SAND

There are few more dramatic examples of the power of the wind than dust storms. Like boiling walls of sand, such storms are some of the most unpleasant weather you're likely to find. They're common in the sand deserts of the world, such as the Sahara, but sometimes

occur in areas quite some distance from the deserts. But wherever they occur, they bring all activity to a standstill.

After a long period of drought vegetation on the ground becomes sparser, exposing the soil. If a strong weather system such as a major thunderstorm or frontal system (often the change heralding the end of a heatwave) approaches, turbulent winds may pick up millions of tons of topsoil and whirl them high into the air. Severe wind squalls preceding hurricanes can also whip up formidable dust storms lasting up to 24 hours.

TOWERS OF FLAME

A major, uncontrolled fire, known as wildfire, can be an awesome sight, with flames towering 600 feet (180 m) into the air. And as the dramatic fires in Sydney, Australia, in 1994 demonstrated, wildfire can disrupt the activities of a major city. On this occasion more than 800 separate fires burned over 1.9 million acres (800,000 ha) of land, killing four people, and destroying property worth millions of dollars.

The recipe for wildfire is one part fuel (vegetation and ground litter), three parts weather, and a pinch of something, such as a spark from a carelessly discarded cigarette.

Wildfires are common on every continent where the recipe is met, with the Mediterranean countries and California joining Australia in the high-risk category. All these places experience heatwaves with strong, gusty winds, and the hot, dry, windy weather is likely to produce an outbreak of wildfires.

LEFT: The strongest dust storms, where the visibility drops to zero, may be 2 miles (3 km) tall and travel for thousands of miles. This storm is sweeping across the Sahara Desert. Small cumulus clouds have formed over the most vigorous updrafts of the dust front.

RIGHT: The major wildfires in Sydney, Australia, in January 1994 created a pall of smoke that overhung the city for days. In the past most wildfires were started by lightning strikes, but today the majority of wildfires are caused by people. In major fires turbulent updrafts will lift sparks thousands of feet into the air, carrying them many miles before dropping them on the ground to start new fires.

RIGHT: This wet microburst is showering farmland in Victoria, Australia. From 1975 to 1985 the US National Transportation and Safety Board reported that 149 aircraft accidents in the States, resulting in 450 deaths, were caused by wind shear, principally from microbursts such as this one.

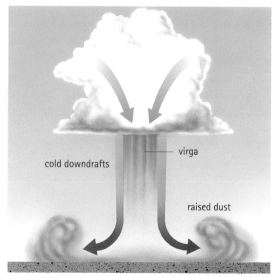

FORMATION OF A DRY MICROBURST
Cold air accelerating downward from a cloud hits the ground and spreads rapidly away from its touchdown point. Rain evaporating in mid-air forms virga.

THE TERROR OF THE TROPICS: HURRICANES

Hurricanes are nature's most deadly storms: immensely powerful and destructive, they can cause great loss of life and damage if they hit land or cross shipping lanes. Known as hurricanes in North America and the Caribbean, tropical cyclones in the Indian Ocean and Southwest Pacific, and typhoons in Southeast Asia, these are all the same phenomenon—intense, low-pressure, rapidly rotating storm systems. They form only in the tropics, drawing their energy from the warmth of tropical oceans.

TROPICAL TURMOIL

Storms become tropical cyclones and typhoons once they produce sustained gale-force winds blowing at 39 miles per hour (63 km/h) or more. In North America these cyclones are called tropical storms until their sustained wind speed reaches 74 miles per hour (119 km/h). Then they are upgraded to hurricane status. Since the 1970s weather services have used an alphabetical system of alternating female and male names for hurricanes.

On any one day there are thousands of thunderstorms in the tropics, triggered by the strong heating effects of the sun. Certain conditions alert forecasters to the possibility that a tropical storm is forming. These conditions include clusters of thunderstorms over the ocean that last for 48 hours, a sea-surface temperature warmer than 80°F (26.5°C), and relatively light winds throughout the depth of the troposphere. If, over the next couple of days, the thunderstorms start to take on the characteristic shape of curved lines of cloud swirling into a low-pressure system, a hurricane may be about to form. The Coriolis effect (see page 24) causes the storms to take on this shape and start to rotate.

Thunderstorms in these spiral bands, which are known as feeder bands, act like energy pumps, converting heat from the ocean into rotational energy. Usually, air pressure at the surface falls rapidly, generating more thunderstorms, and the hurricane continues to intensify until there is a balance between the energy feeding in at the base of the hurricane and the energy exiting higher up.

A hurricane may intensify with frightening speed. Fully formed, it is an awesome sight: spiral bands of towering cumulonimbus clouds swirling inward until they converge and form a band of clouds, known as the eye wall, around the center of the hurricane. Rippled sheets of cirrostratus clouds from the merged tops of the thunderstorms stream away from the eye, or center, of the hurricane.

Because these storms' rotation is caused by the Coriolis effect, they cannot exist less than 6° north or south of the Equator. They are normally most intense between the 15° and 20° latitudes and tend to move farther from the Equator as they age. They rarely survive once they are more than 30° from the Equator, because ocean temperatures become too cold to sustain them and upper-level westerly winds literally tear them apart.

Some tropical storms may survive for up to 14 days, making them the longest lived of the low-pressure systems. The largest reach a diameter of about 300 miles (480 km) and travel over thousands of miles of ocean.

A DANGER TO LIFE

The dangers of hurricanes are many. Unlike tornadoes, most of which pass by in a matter of minutes and leave behind a narrow path of destruction, hurricanes typically take several hours to pass by and may seriously affect up to 60 miles (100 km) of coastline at a time. The feeder bands of a hurricane may spawn several tornadoes, further increasing the devastation. Although feared for their devastating winds, hurricanes also bring torrential rain and flooding, and more people worldwide lose their lives in floods than from the damage caused by winds.

Flooding may be made worse by the storm surge, or storm tide, which accompanies a hurricane landfall. As the storm approaches land, strong winds blowing toward the shore pile water up on the coastline. The very low pressure near the center of the hurricane also causes the water level beneath the storm to rise, rather like water being sucked up a straw. These storm surges may raise the sea level by 10 to 13 feet (3 to 4 m) or more. And the sea level may rise even higher if the hurricane crosses the coast at the time of the normal high tide or if the ocean floor forms a valley that leads into funnel-shaped bays, thereby allowing the hurricane's giant waves to pound towns normally protected by reefs and sea walls.

Since before the time of the great Mongol warrior Kublai Khan, who lost his invasion fleet to a typhoon off Japan in the 13th century,

ABOVE: These palm trees on Plantation Island, in Fiji, have been damaged by a severe tropical cyclone. This picture was taken about 24 hours after the cyclone passed by.

The eye wall is where the strongest winds are found and sustained speeds of 155 miles per hour (250 km/h), gusting to 185 miles per hour (300 km/h), have been measured. Yet the wind dies away rapidly only a few miles closer to the center. The eye of a hurricane, where surface pressures are lowest, has light winds and may be relatively clear of cloud in the most intense storms.

INSIDE A HURRICANE
Tropical oceans are the life-blood of hurricanes. Towering thunderstorms draw energy from the ocean surface high up into the atmosphere, feeding the hurricane. Near the surface, winds strengthen as they spiral toward the calm eye, only to rise and spin out of the top of the hurricane. These devastating storms can be 200 to 300 miles (320 to 480 km) in diameter.

mariners have feared hurricanes more than any other storms. Storm-force winds accompanied by towering waves up to 65 feet (20 m) high, may whip up in just a few hours. Even the largest oceangoing vessels try to avoid hurricanes if given sufficient warning.

TRACKING THE STORM

A hurricane may provide some clues to its presence. In most cases the ocean swell rises rapidly ahead of it. Dense cirrostratus clouds spiraling out of the top of the hurricane fill the sky. The atmospheric pressure drops close to 1,000 hectopascals before the gales arrive.

As the hurricane gets closer, winds rapidly become stronger and the pressure drops further. Severe thunderstorms, which may spawn tornadoes (see page 62), often accompany the hurricane's feeder bands. As the hurricane center approaches, the sky is obscured by horizontal rain, and winds grow so strong that no one can move about safely outside.

If people are caught in a storm surge or flooding, their chances of survival are not good. The Philippines is the most hurricane-prone nation on earth, but tales of devastation are common in almost every country that has a tropical ocean bordering its shores.

LEFT: In dollar terms, the most expensive hurricane to date was Hurricane Andrew in the United States, which devastated southern Florida, Louisiana, and parts of Texas in August 1992. The damage bill was estimated to be approximately $30 billion. This ruined house was located in Florida, south of Miami.

ABOVE: *This photograph of*
Hurricane Elena was taken by
the Space Shuttle Discovery
in 1985. Elena passed over
Cuba before reaching the
Gulf of Mexico.
INSET: *A color-enhanced*
satellite image of Hurricane
Andrew in the Gulf of Mexico
in 1992.

Countries affected by hurricanes have established sophisticated warning systems to protect their inhabitants. Meteorologists use satellites (see page 122) to monitor the development and movement of storms over the open ocean. Once the storms are closer to land, weather radar (see page 122) accurately pinpoint their often erratic path. Automatic weather stations (see page 124) on remote islands and reefs gather vital information on the strength of the storms. In some areas specially strengthened aircraft fly into the very heart of the storm to take readings of wind speed and air pressure (see page 125). In recent years the combination of these systems, supported by experienced forecasters, has significantly reduced the deaths caused by hurricanes (see page 132).

In the United States a five-point rating scale, called the Saffir–Simpson scale, is applied to hurricanes. This ranges from category 1 storms, which produce minimal damage, through category 3 storms, which produce extensive damage, to catastrophic category 5 storms, such as Hurricane Camille, which killed 256 people along the Gulf coast and in the Virginias in 1969. This hurricane produced a storm tide of 24.6 feet (7.5 m).

SEASONS IN THE TROPICS: MONSOONS

Monsoons (from the Arabic word *mausim*, meaning *season*) was the name originally given to the two main wind systems that occur in the Arabian Sea: the northeast winds of the cool season and the southwest winds of the wet, summer season. Today meteorologists use the term more widely to describe the seasonal changes in tropical regions (see map on facing page). The southwest monsoon of southern Asia is the most dramatic, and its arrival marks an abrupt change in the weather from dry conditions to torrential rain.

SIBERIA IS THE SOURCE

There is a close relationship between Siberia's winter weather and the monsoons of Southeast Asia and Australia. During winter in the Northern Hemisphere cold air accumulates over Siberia to form the world's largest high-pressure system. The strength of the monsoons is partly determined by the intensity of this system, which produces strengthening northeast trade winds over central and southern Asia.

High-pressure systems are strongest when there is a cold surface beneath their center, such as the extreme cold over Siberia. The Coriolis effect (see page 24) causes the strong winds from this high to blow from the northeast. This is the northeast monsoon, bringing cool, dry weather to the Indian subcontinent.

These winds are deflected by the Coriolis effect once they cross the Equator, and they then become the moist, unstable northwest monsoon that brings the wet season to northern Australia and the tropical islands of the southern Indian Ocean and the Coral Sea. This monsoon is rather like a gigantic sea breeze (see page 44) that lasts for months, rather than hours. It blows from cooler areas to warmer ones, picking up moisture when it blows over warm seas.

As the northern summer approaches (about May), the Siberian high-pressure system collapses, while the high-pressure systems in

RIGHT: Monsoon rains near Goa, on the west coast of India, feed this mighty waterfall and swell streams that were mere trickles in the dry season, replenishing water supplies for the dry months ahead.

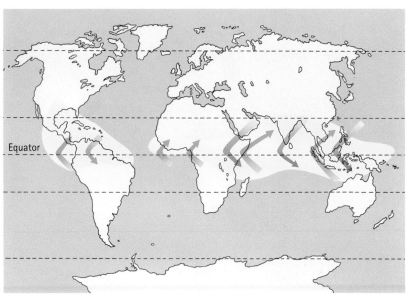

MONSOON AREAS

The main monsoon areas straddle the Equator. The green arrows show the winds that produce the southwest summer monsoon in the north. The red arrows indicate the winds that produce the northeast monsoon in the northern winter, which becomes the northwest summer monsoon across the Equator.

BELOW: *This man in Porbandar, on the west coast of India, is trying to save his sewing machine from the chest-high monsoon floods.*

the Southern Hemisphere strengthen and shift northward. A series of low-pressure systems forms north of the Equator, with centers usually located over the Arabian peninsula, north-central India, and the South China Sea. The southeast trade winds in the Southern Hemisphere strengthen and, because of the Coriolis effect, become southwesterly after they surge across the Equator toward these lows. This is the southwest monsoon, which is responsible for some of the heaviest rain in the world, particularly over the Himalayas (see page 72).

MONSOON FLOODS

Typhoons and tropical cyclones, which can cause catastrophic flooding if they reach land (see page 67), are more likely to occur in the monsoon season. Some of the most extreme floods have occurred in the Ganges Delta, in Bangladesh, with tens of thousands of people drowned and millions made homeless.

The intensity of the monsoons around the world is linked to El Niño (see page 36). The monsoonal circulation is not only responsible for floods, though, because floods in one area are linked to droughts in other regions.

There could be devastating consequences if any of the world's monsoons failed to arrive. A weak southwest monsoon, for instance, can have particularly dire effects, because half the world's population relies on the monsoon rain for vital water supplies. From the mountainous southwest of Arabia, to the Indian subcontinent and southeast China, crops need the monsoon rains if they are to flourish, and lack of rainfall means poor crops and famine for millions of people. Such is the wide-reaching power of the monsoon.

IT'S A RECORD! WEATHER EXTREMES

People have been telling tales about incredible weather for thousands of years, but usually there is scant evidence to support such stories. With a few exceptions, no reliable records of the weather were kept until the early 20th century. Extreme events seldom occur where there are meteorological instruments, and even when there *are* such instruments present, extreme weather may well cause them to fail. When researchers do manage to measure these events, though, the enormous power of the weather is revealed.

COLDER THAN COLD, HOTTER THAN HOT

It should come as no great surprise that Vostok, high on the Antarctic plateau at 11,220 feet (3,420 m), holds the record for the world's lowest temperature of minus 128.6°F (–89.2°C),

which was recorded in midwinter on July 21, 1983. The temperature on the Antarctic plateau is low all year around; for instance, Antarctic Plateau Station's average temperature is minus 70°F (–57°C). By contrast, Siberia, a vast region in eastern Russia, has the world's greatest annual temperature variation. Verkhoyansk, for example, experiences temperatures that range from minus 90°F (–68°C) in winter to 98°F (37°C) in summer, a huge difference of 188°F (105°C).

The Sahara Desert belt, which stretches across North Africa to the Arabian peninsula, is consistently the hottest region on earth. The small mining settlement at Dallol, in Ethiopia, averaged a daytime temperature of 94°F (34°C) between 1960 and 1966. The Libyan town of Al'Aziziyah is also in this broad desert belt, and

ABOVE: The stark beauty of the Valley of the Moon, in Chile's Atacama Desert, belies its record low rainfall. Much of the west coast of Chile, where this desert is located, is extremely arid because the persistent easterly winds lose their moisture as they cross the Andes.

RIGHT: Antarctica is the world's coldest continent. Vast expanses of sea ice remain frozen throughout the year. Here people on an expedition are walking on the ice on the Ross Sea.

BELOW: The island of Kauai, in Hawaii, holds the record for the greatest number of wet days per year. Cumulus clouds obscure the top of the Ka'a'alahina Ridge.

it recorded the world's highest shade temperature of 136°F (58°C) on September 13, 1922. Not far behind is Death Valley, where a temperature of 134°F (56.7°C), on July 10, 1913, was the highest ever recorded in the United States. From July 6 to August 17, 1917, Death Valley had a run of 43 consecutive days when the temperature exceeded 120°F (49°C).

COME RAIN OR SHINE

Stories of huge hailstones are like tales of the fish that got away: the stones that are collected and measured are always smaller than those that escaped. The heaviest authenticated hailstones weighed up to 2 pounds 3 ounces (1 kg) and fell in the Gopalganj district of Bangladesh on April 14, 1986, killing 92 people.

The lament "It always rains on weekends" is undoubtedly true at Mount Waialeale, on the island of Kauai, Hawaii, where it rains on average 350 days of the year. Mawsynram, in India, although it has fewer wet days, accumulates 467½ inches (11,874 mm) in a typical year, and is the wettest place in the world.

This is a huge contrast to Chile's Atacama Desert, where it virtually never rains. The town of Arica averages less than $\frac{1}{250}$ inch (0.1 mm) per year. A little damper but very sunny is Yuma, in the United States, which has an average of 4,055 hours of sunshine per year and only 401 hours of cloud.

WELL, BLOW ME DOWN!

Most instruments that measure wind speed fail or produce suspect readings in the strongest winds, so damage estimates are often the best indication of the true wind speed. Because of the ferocious winds tornadoes produce (see page 62), their strength is very difficult to measure. A reading of 280 miles per hour (450 km/h) at Wichita Falls, in the United States, on April 2, 1958, is the highest documented wind speed.

Aside from tornadic winds, a record gust of 231 miles per hour (371 km/h) was measured at Mount Washington, in the United States, on April 12, 1934. Closer to sea level, Thule, in Greenland, recorded a wind speed of 207 miles per hour (333 km/h) on March 8, 1972.

HARNESSING NATURAL ENERGY

Powered by atomic fusion, the incandescent sun continually bathes the earth with radiation, which causes the winds that blow ceaselessly around the globe (see page 22). These winds generate the waves that pound our shores and bring the rains that replenish our lakes and rivers (see page 34). Given the problems caused by using fossil fuels and nuclear energy, people have recently made increased efforts to better utilize the enormous natural energy in our weather.

WIND POWER AND PLANT POWER

People have harnessed the power of the wind for hundreds of years. Sailing ships, which were the main form of sea transport until steam ships were invented in the 1800s, were propelled by the wind. Since the 12th century windmills have pumped water, ground grain, and powered machines, and, since the early 20th century, produced electricity. The use of windmills declined significantly in the 1940s once coal- and oil-burning power plants became common, but the 1970s saw a renewed interest in wind power.

By the mid-1990s wind-powered turbines had become a cost-effective and nonpolluting form of renewable energy. These turbines can power farms or homes, and dozens can be linked up to supply electricity to densely populated areas. The United States currently produces enough wind-generated energy to meet the residential needs of a million people. The California wind farms at Altamont Pass, Palm Springs, and Tehachapi are the three largest US installations.

Plants use sunlight, carbon dioxide, and rainwater to grow. We use some of the renewable energy stored in plants, known as biomass energy, as fuel. Wood is the main source of biomass energy, but some other plant materials used for fuel are far less polluting than wood and nonrenewable energy sources such as fossil fuels. For example, agronomists have developed various crops that produce liquid fuels, including ethanol and methanol. These can power internal combustion engines. Scientists have also developed a technique to capture methane gas from waste material,

including landfills, and generate power with it. In the United States there are approximately 100 power plants in 31 states that generate electricity from landfill methane.

WATER, WAVE, AND SUN

The ancient Egyptians were the first people to employ water power: to turn stones for grinding grain. Today the Egyptians generate much of their electricity with water from the Aswan Dam. Hydroelectricity, as it's known, is now a major source of power on every conti-

ABOVE: Wind turbines are able to meet a large proportion of the local community's needs wherever the annual wind speed averages more than 12½ miles per hour (20 km/h). These wind turbines are in Altamont Pass, Calilfornia.

nent except Antarctica and it supplies about a quarter of the world's electricity. Brazil has the world's largest hydroelectric power station, and this and other smaller dams supply 90 percent of the country's power.

Covering 70 percent of the earth's surface, the oceans hold huge reserves of kinetic and thermal energy. Only a tiny fraction of this potential has been utilized, but two processes hold promise. One is the conversion of wave energy into electric power. A system of wave-driven turbines installed by Norway operates in the North Sea. The second process involves generating electricity from the temperature difference between the warm surface waters of the tropical ocean and the cold waters beneath. The technique is called ocean thermal energy conversion (OTEC), and a prototype plant in Hawaii is the leading example.

A virtually infinite supply of energy pours down on the earth in the form of sunshine (solar radiation). Solar radiation is the ultimate nonpolluting, renewable energy source, but until recently it has been difficult and costly to convert into electricity. Technologies are improving rapidly, however, and solar radiation is now a viable power source, particularly in remote, sunny places that are not connected to the main electricity grid.

Solar panels capture solar radiation and convert it to electricity. They can power a range of instruments, such as satellites, telephones, automobiles, and automatic weather stations (see page 124). Large-scale solar-power plants concentrate solar radiation for use as the heat source for steam engines.

RIGHT: *The United States Luz International plant, in southern California, is the world's largest solar-power plant. It generates enough power to supply a city with more than 350,000 people.*

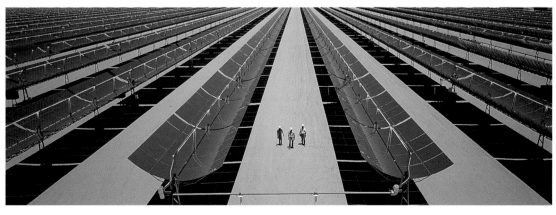

WEATHER-WATCHER'S GUIDE

By learning to identify clouds
and other weather phenomena, we can
greatly increase our knowledge of
the weather and also achieve some skill
in forecasting, one of humankind's
oldest endeavors.

HOW TO USE THE WEATHER-WATCHER'S GUIDE

The Weather-Watcher's Guide is a practical introduction to observing the weather. Once we can identify different weather phenomena, and know which physical processes have formed them, the way we view the weather and its many manifestations is transformed.

Instead of finding the weather simply confusing, we can begin to make sense of the kaleidoscope of natural phenomena. By observing and identifying weather events, and taking into account information provided by media forecasts, we can start to put in place some of the pieces of the colossal jigsaw puzzle that is the weather.

The following guide consists of six sections (see below left), each containing a number of text entries. Each entry covers a specific weather phenomenon and is divided by headings into six or seven blocks of text described on the opposite page.

COLORED BANDING

The guide is divided into six sections according to the major groups of weather phenomena. The colored banding across the top of the entry indicates which section that entry belongs to.

FOG

DEW AND FROST

CLOUDS

PRECIPITATION

STORMS

OPTICAL EFFECTS

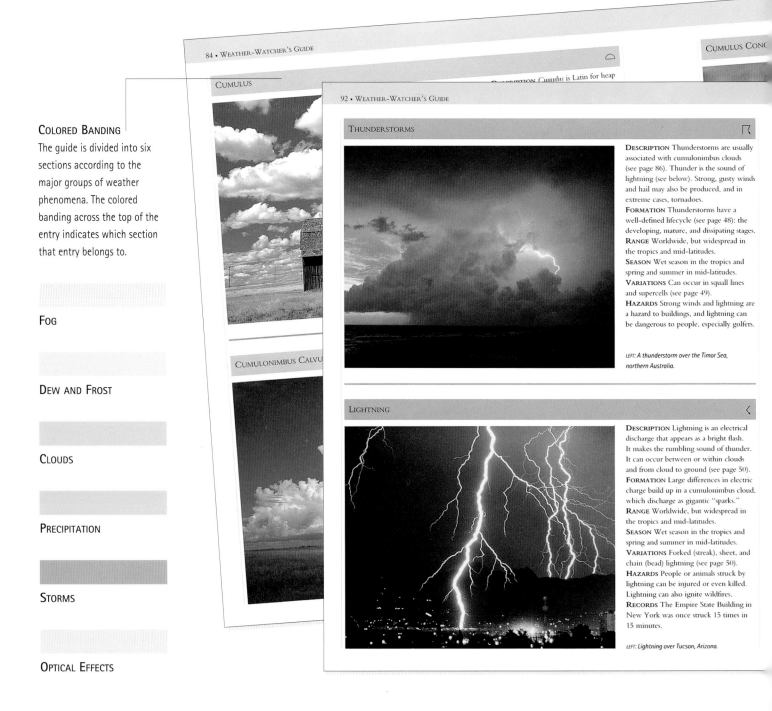

84 • WEATHER-WATCHER'S GUIDE

CUMULUS CONC

CUMULUS

DESCRIPTION *Cumulus* is Latin for heap

CUMULONIMBUS CALVU

92 • WEATHER-WATCHER'S GUIDE

THUNDERSTORMS

DESCRIPTION Thunderstorms are usually associated with cumulonimbus clouds (see page 86). Thunder is the sound of lightning (see below). Strong, gusty winds and hail may also be produced, and in extreme cases, tornadoes.
FORMATION Thunderstorms have a well-defined lifecycle (see page 48): the developing, mature, and dissipating stages.
RANGE Worldwide, but widespread in the tropics and mid-latitudes.
SEASON Wet season in the tropics and spring and summer in mid-latitudes.
VARIATIONS Can occur in squall lines and supercells (see page 49).
HAZARDS Strong winds and lightning are a hazard to buildings, and lightning can be dangerous to people, especially golfers.

LEFT: *A thunderstorm over the Timor Sea, northern Australia.*

LIGHTNING

DESCRIPTION Lightning is an electrical discharge that appears as a bright flash. It makes the rumbling sound of thunder. It can occur between or within clouds and from cloud to ground (see page 50).
FORMATION Large differences in electric charge build up in a cumulonimbus cloud, which discharge as gigantic "sparks."
RANGE Worldwide, but widespread in the tropics and mid-latitudes.
SEASON Wet season in the tropics and spring and summer in mid-latitudes.
VARIATIONS Forked (streak), sheet, and chain (bead) lightning (see page 50).
HAZARDS People or animals struck by lightning can be injured or even killed. Lightning can also ignite wildfires.
RECORDS The Empire State Building in New York was once struck 15 times in 15 minutes.

LEFT: *Lightning over Tucson, Arizona.*

TITLE OF ENTRY
For more information on the different weather phenomena, refer to the preceding chapters.

CLOUDS • 85

STORMS • 93

TEXT ENTRIES:
DESCRIPTION Describes the physical appearance of the phenomenon. It supplements the information provided in the photograph.

FORMATION Explains the physical processes that cause the phenomenon. Many of these processes are described in more detail in the preceding chapters, and the relevant pages are cross-referenced where appropriate.

RANGE Indicates the main areas of the world where the phenomenon occurs.

SEASON Outlines any seasonal patterns across the range of the phenomenon.

VARIATIONS Notes different forms that the phenomenon may take, as well as any differences in terminology around the world.

HAZARDS Lists any potentially hazardous conditions produced by the phenomenon, such as dangers it may pose to shipping or aviation.

RECORDS Recounts any extreme events of the phenomenon that have been recorded. The majority of records included here are from *The Guinness Book of Records*; other records were provided by various national weather services. Refer to pages 72–3 for more information on weather extremes.

TORNADOES

DESCRIPTION A tornado is a grayish funnel, usually about 450 feet (135 m) across, dangling from the base of a thunderstorm. It may move slowly or at up to 60 miles per hour (100 km/h).
FORMATION It's produced by severe thunderstorms when a funnel descends from the cloud, or develops near the surface and extends upward (see page 62).
RANGE Mainly in mid-latitudes.
SEASON Spring and summer.
VARIATIONS Classified by strength (see page 63), with F5 being the most severe.
HAZARDS Wind speeds up to 300 miles per hour (500 km/h) destroy any structure in the tornado's path.
RECORDS The longest path ever taken by a tornado was a 293-mile (471 km) rampage on May 26, 1917, stretching from Matoon, Illinois, to Charleston, Indiana.

RIGHT: A tornado near Laverne, Oklahoma.

PHOTOGRAPH
An image of the phenomenon (or, in some cases, its effects) is included to help the weather-watcher identify the event in the field.

WATERSPOUTS

DESCRIPTION These are like tornadoes over water (see above), but are generally much less intense and usually not associated with thunderstorms. They may produce a plume of spray where the base touches the water.
FORMATION Waterspouts form when winds rotating near the surface interact with the updraft of a cumulus cloud.
RANGE Generally tropical and subtropical coastal waters.
SEASON Vary widely around the world.
VARIATIONS Wind speeds vary from light to about 100 miles per hour (160 km/h).
HAZARDS Stronger waterspouts pose a hazard to small boats.
RECORDS The tallest measured waterspout occurred off the coast of New South Wales, Australia, on May 16, 1898; it was 5,014 feet (1,528 m) tall.

RIGHT: A waterspout off the Costa Brava, Spain.

INTERNATIONAL WEATHER SYMBOL
Many, but not all, weather phenomena are designated by an internationally recognized weather symbol (see page 131). This symbol is included, where appropriate.

CAPTION TO PHOTOGRAPH
The caption may include information about where the photograph was taken.

RADIATION FOG

DESCRIPTION Radiation fog is cloud on the ground.

FORMATION Generally, it forms on clear, still nights when heat from the earth's surface is radiated back out to space and the ground cools significantly. This in turn cools a layer of air near the ground, and moisture in the layer condenses into billions of tiny water droplets.

RANGE Worldwide except in desert areas.

SEASON Varies widely around the world.

HAZARDS Poses a hazard to aviation and motorists as it reduces visibility markedly.

LEFT: Radiation fog over Latrigg, Cumbria, England.

ADVECTION FOG

DESCRIPTION Advection fog is low-level cloud that can form over land or sea.

FORMATION It forms when moist air drifts into a colder environment, or when cold air drifts into a moist environment. This movement of air is called advection.

RANGE Worldwide except in inland deserts.

SEASON Varies widely around the world.

VARIATIONS Sea fog often forms when moist air above a warm current drifts over colder ocean water. Steam fog results when cold air passes over warm water.

HAZARDS Poses a hazard to many forms of transportation, including shipping, as it reduces visibility.

RECORDS The foggiest place in the United States is Cape Disappointment, Washington, which averages 106 days of fog every year.

LEFT: Advection fog off the west coast of Sweden.

UPSLOPE FOG

DESCRIPTION Upslope fog is cloud on or close to the ground.

FORMATION It forms when moist air moves over rising, or upslope, ground. The air is lifted and cooled, which leads to condensation.

RANGE Common over hilly or mountainous areas, particularly on high ground close to the sea, where the surrounding air usually contains a significant amount of water vapor.

SEASON Varies widely around the world.

HAZARDS It reduces visibility markedly. Poses a hazard to aviation as it can mask hills and mountains from pilots' view.

RIGHT: Upslope fog in the Blue Mountains, New South Wales, Australia.

FOG STRATUS

DESCRIPTION Fog stratus is a bank of very low cloud. It's usually quite thin but can cover an extensive area.

FORMATION Usually, it forms in the early morning when a bank of radiation fog rises as the sun begins to heat the ground. The fog bank shrinks, starting from the edges and the base.

RANGE Worldwide except in desert areas.

SEASON Varies widely around the world.

VARIATIONS Low cloud drifting on to nearby hills and mountains can be described as fog stratus, although this is actually cloud on the ground rather than lifting fog.

HAZARDS Poses a hazard to aviation as it can mask hills and mountains from pilots' view.

RIGHT: Fog stratus over Keswick, Cumbria, England.

DEW

DESCRIPTION Dew is a collection of water droplets that form on surfaces at or near ground level. It may appear on leaves, grass, and even spiders' webs. It forms at night and usually evaporates by early to mid-morning.

FORMATION It's formed by a layer of air close to the ground being cooled overnight, causing water vapor to condense on low-level surfaces. The conditions for dew to form are very similar to those for radiation fog (see page 80), and the two often occur together.

RANGE Worldwide, especially in coastal areas, where the air is usually moist.

SEASON Varies widely around the world.

HAZARDS Poses a hazard to motorists as it can cause roads to become slippery.

LEFT: Dew drops on a flower's stamens.

FROST

DESCRIPTION Frost is a layer of ice crystals that covers the ground, vegetation, and other surfaces. It forms at night and normally melts by mid-morning, but can last much longer in extreme cold.

FORMATION The temperature of a surface must fall to 32°F (0°C) or below for frost to form. Frost results either when dew freezes (hoar frost) or when water vapor immediately freezes to ice (without first becoming liquid) after contact with a cold surface (rime frost).

RANGE Worldwide but only at high altitudes in the tropics.

SEASON All year, especially in winter.

VARIATIONS Appearance varies depending on the underlying surface.

HAZARDS Poses a hazard to motorists when it causes roads to become slippery. Damages fruit trees and vegetables.

LEFT: Frost on a windowpane.

STRATUS

DESCRIPTION Stratus is a low-level cloud that may appear in isolated tufts or as an extensive, ragged deck. It can be low enough to cover hills, mountains, or tall buildings.

FORMATION It forms when condensation occurs at low levels, usually because of high humidity in the lower atmosphere, or when air is lifted by hills or mountains.

RANGE Worldwide but most common in mountainous areas near the ocean. Occurs anywhere from 0 to 6,500 feet (1,950 m).

SEASON All year.

VARIATIONS Nimbostratus (rain-bearing) occurs when precipitation falls from stratus. See also fog stratus (page 81).

HAZARDS Poses a hazard to aviation as it can mask hills and mountains from pilots' view.

RIGHT: Stratus cloud over Karitane, New Zealand.

STRATOCUMULUS

DESCRIPTION Stratocumulus usually appears as ragged and ill-defined tufts that don't grow much vertically. It can occur in isolated pockets or extensive decks covering hundreds of square miles.

FORMATION It forms when air is lifted and condensation occurs in the lower atmosphere. The lifting mechanism is usually weak, and can be produced by turbulence on the ground or by gentle convection.

RANGE Very common worldwide. Occurs anywhere from 2,000 to 6,000 feet (600 to 1,800 m).

SEASON All year.

RIGHT: Stratocumulus cloud over the Gascoyne region, Western Australia.

CUMULUS

DESCRIPTION *Cumulus* is Latin for heap and cumulus clouds indeed look like individual heaps in the sky.

FORMATION Cumulus is formed by weak convection (see page 40), so the cloud doesn't grow much vertically.

RANGE Very common worldwide, over both land and sea. Occurs anywhere, typically from 2,000 to 4,000 feet (600 to 1,200 m).

SEASON All year; probably more common over land in summer.

VARIATIONS Cumulus humilis is broader than it's high, and cumulus mediocris is as tall as it's wide. Pyrocumulus forms when the convection is caused by wildfire.

LEFT: Cumulus cloud over western Washington.

CUMULONIMBUS CALVUS

DESCRIPTION This spectacular cloud extends from the lower atmosphere to the top of the troposphere. It produces showers and occasionally snow.

FORMATION It forms when powerful convection is present together with atmospheric instability (see page 41). It starts as a basic cumulus cloud, and progresses to cumulus congestus (see facing page) before becoming cumulonimbus calvus.

RANGE Worldwide but most frequent in the tropics. Typically extends from about 2,000 to 30,000 feet (600 to 9,000 m).

SEASON All year in tropics, but common in spring and summer in mid-latitudes.

VARIATIONS Can progress to the thunderstorm stage, cumulonimbus (see page 86).

HAZARDS Produces moderate to severe turbulence for aircraft.

LEFT: A cumulonimbus calvus cloud over the Northern Territory, Australia.

CUMULUS CONGESTUS

DESCRIPTION This cumulus cloud is taller than it is wide, and is often a brilliant white in the upper levels. It can produce showers, sometimes heavy, and occasionally snow in cold temperatures.

FORMATION It forms when vigorous convection is present together with atmospheric instability (see page 41).

RANGE Worldwide but most common in the tropics. Typically extends from about 2,000 to 20,000 feet (600 to 6,000 m).

SEASON All year.

VARIATIONS Can occur over ocean, when it's sometimes referred to as maritime cumulus congestus.

HAZARDS Can produce moderate turbulence for aircraft.

ABOVE: Cumulus congestus cloud over the Northern Territory, Australia.

CUMULONIMBUS INCUS WITH ANVIL

DESCRIPTION This cloud produces thunderstorms. It has the shape of a black-smith's anvil and is crowned with a vast, wedge-shaped formation of ice crystals.

FORMATION It forms when powerful convection is present together with marked atmospheric instability (see page 41).

RANGE Worldwide except high Arctic and Antarctic zones. Extends from about 3,000 to 35,000 feet (900 to 10,500 m) in mid-latitudes and can extend as high as 65,000 feet (19,500 m) in the tropics.

SEASON Most frequent in tropical wet season and during spring and summer in mid-latitudes.

VARIATIONS Can produce hail, micro-bursts, and tornadoes in extreme cases.

HAZARDS Poses a hazard to aviation as it can cause turbulence, icing, and hail.

LEFT: A cumulonimbus incus cloud with anvil over Darwin, the Northern Territory, Australia.

ALTOSTRATUS

DESCRIPTION This cloud occurs in the middle troposphere, and is typically a fairly featureless deck that may be thin enough to see through, or a very thick, rain- and snow-producing cloud.

FORMATION It's produced when moist air at mid-levels of the troposphere is lifted, often by a frontal system (see page 26). It can be very extensive, covering thousands of square miles.

RANGE Worldwide but more common in mid- and high latitudes than in the tropics. Occurs anywhere from 6,500 to 16,500 feet (1,950 to 4,950 m).

SEASON All year but especially in winter.

VARIATIONS The undulatus formation produces a wavelike, or "rippled," effect.

HAZARDS Can cause aircraft wings to ice over.

LEFT: Altostratus cloud over Kangaroo Valley, New South Wales, Australia.

ALTOCUMULUS

DESCRIPTION Altocumulus occurs in the middle troposphere and can extend over a large area. It's frequently associated with an approaching frontal system (see page 26), and can produce light showers or snow. It's often mixed with altostratus (see facing page).

FORMATION It's produced by air being lifted in the middle troposphere and by some atmospheric instability (see page 41).

RANGE Worldwide but more common in mid- and high latitudes than in the tropics. Occurs anywhere from 6,500 to 16,500 feet (1,950 to 4,950 m).

SEASON All year but especially in winter.

VARIATIONS Can appear as a wavelike formation (undulatus), turretlike (castellanus), and like fish scales (mackerel sky).

HAZARDS Poses a hazard to aviation as it can cause turbulence and icing.

RIGHT: *Altocumulus clouds tinged pink at sunset.*

ALTOCUMULUS LENTICULARIS

DESCRIPTION Altocumulus lenticularis is one of the most fascinating clouds for weather watchers. It's a smooth, elongated cloud with a lenslike shape, which may remain stationary for a long time.

FORMATION It forms when moist air is lifted and shaped by mountain waves (see page 32).

RANGE Worldwide in mountainous regions. Occurs anywhere from 6,500 to 16,500 feet (1,950 to 4,950 m).

SEASON Varies widely, depending on the location of the mountains.

VARIATIONS Can appear as a "flying-saucer" shape and has probably been responsible for many UFO reports.

HAZARDS Mountain waves can produce severe turbulence for aircraft.

RIGHT: *Altocumulus lenticularis cloud over Denali, Alaska.*

CIRRUS

DESCRIPTION Cirrus clouds appear in the upper atmosphere as elongated wisps of cloud. *Cirrus* is Latin for tuft of hair and many cirrus formations do resemble this. It can appear in isolation or as large sheets across the sky, which can indicate an approaching frontal system (see page 26).

FORMATION Cirrus clouds form at great heights, well above the freezing level, and are composed of billions of ice crystals. Strong winds at these levels often lead to long streamers of cirrus forming across the sky.

RANGE Worldwide. Occurs above 16,500 feet (4,950 m).

SEASON All year.

VARIATIONS Can appear as hooklike streamers (cirrus uncinus) or as a wavelike formation (cirrus undulatus).

LEFT: *Cirrus clouds tinted gold at sunset.*

CIRROCUMULUS

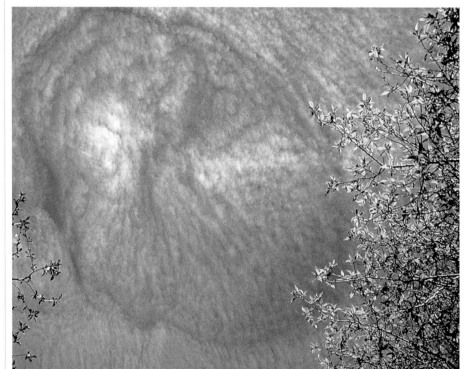

DESCRIPTION Cirrocumulus is one of the more unusual cloud formations. It appears as a cirrus cloud with "texture," which may be ripples or more intricate, wave-like formations.

FORMATION Atmospheric instability (see page 41) at the level where the cloud is forming produces a more "clumped" appearance than the long streamers of cirrostratus (see facing page). It can be isolated or very extensive in area.

RANGE Worldwide. Occurs above 16,500 feet (4,950 m).

SEASON All year.

VARIATIONS Can appear as a wavelike form (undulatus), with a series of finely structured ripples sometimes extending right across the sky.

LEFT: *Cirrocumulus cloud over Boulder, Colorado.*

CIRROSTRATUS

2

DESCRIPTION Cirrostratus can produce some very attractive-looking skies, particularly when it is tinged with pink near sunrise or sunset. Cirrostratus usually appears as very extensive, layered streamers across the sky, running almost parallel to each other. When elongated streamers extend across much of the sky, meteorologists sometimes refer to the formation as jet-stream cirrus.

FORMATION The long and streaky appearance is often produced by strong and steady high-level winds, sometimes jet streams (see page 25).

RANGE Worldwide. Occurs above 16,500 feet (4,950 m).

SEASON All year.

VARIATIONS Cirrostratus radiatus appears to converge to one point on the horizon. Very thin cirrostratus can produce optical effects such as haloes and sundogs (see pages 97 and 98).

ABOVE: Strands of cirrostratus streak across the sky.

RAIN AND DRIZZLE

LEFT: A rain shower falling from a cumulonimbus cloud in the Northern Territory, Australia.

DESCRIPTION Rain is liquid water droplets falling from clouds. Drizzle consists of more numerous but smaller droplets than rain, and drizzle droplets fall more slowly than raindrops.

FORMATION Rain forms either when ice crystals falling though a cloud melt to become liquid water droplets, or when liquid water droplets combine to form droplets large enough to reach the ground (see page 46).

RANGE Worldwide but rare in polar regions.

SEASON All year.

VARIATIONS Freezing rain (see below).

HAZARDS Heavy rain can lead to flooding.

RECORDS The "rainiest" place on earth is Mount Waialeale, on the island of Kauai, Hawaii, which averages 350 days of rain every year.

FREEZING RAIN

LEFT: Glaze on plant stems.

DESCRIPTION This consists of supercooled water droplets that freeze at or near the ground. It can produce ice pellets, known as sleet, or a smooth coating of ice on surface objects, known as glaze (see page 55).

FORMATION Freezing rain forms when supercooled water droplets fall from a cloud through air that's below freezing, or meet a surface that's below or near freezing.

RANGE Generally mid- to high latitudes.

SEASON All year in high latitudes; mainly winter in mid-latitudes.

VARIATIONS A mixture of rain and snow may also be referred to as *sleet*.

HAZARDS Creates slippery conditions for vehicles and pedestrians.

RECORDS In Connecticut during the winter of 1969 glaze remained on trees for about six weeks.

SNOW

DESCRIPTION Snow is a falling mass of ice crystals that covers the ground with a white blanket. It may be dry and powdery or wet and "sticky."

FORMATION Snow forms when water vapor in a cloud freezes and forms ice crystals. These crystals descend and combine to form snowflakes, which become heavy enough to reach the ground (see page 46).

RANGE Worldwide, but confined to high altitudes in the tropics.

SEASON All year but usually in winter.

VARIATIONS An infinite number: no two snowflakes are the same.

HAZARDS Slippery road conditions; loss of visibililty; avalanches; and extreme cold.

RECORDS On February 7, 1963, 78 inches (198 cm) of snow buried Mile 47 Camp on Alaska's Cooper River.

RIGHT: *A heavy snowfall covers the ground in New Britain, Connecticut.*

HAIL

DESCRIPTION Hail is irregularly shaped ice globules (hailstones) falling from a cloud, which tend to bounce off grass and shatter on bitumen and concrete.

FORMATION A hailstone begins as a tiny ice crystal in a cumulonimbus cloud, which grows gradually as it circulates in the cloud.

RANGE Worldwide, but most common in mid-latitudes.

SEASON All year but larger hailstones tend to occur in mid-latitudes in late spring and summer.

VARIATIONS Varies from pea-sized to massive orange-sized missiles.

HAZARDS Large hail is a great hazard to people, animal stock, aviation, and vehicles.

RECORDS In Bangladesh in 1986 a hailstorm generated hailstones weighing more than 2 pounds (1 kg), killing 92 people.

RIGHT: *A hailstorm falling over a plain in Colorado.*

THUNDERSTORMS

DESCRIPTION Thunderstorms are usually associated with cumulonimbus clouds (see page 86). Thunder is the sound of lightning (see below). Strong, gusty winds and hail may also be produced, and in extreme cases, tornadoes.

FORMATION Thunderstorms have a well-defined lifecycle (see page 48): the developing, mature, and dissipating stages.

RANGE Worldwide, but widespread in the tropics and mid-latitudes.

SEASON Wet season in the tropics and spring and summer in mid-latitudes.

VARIATIONS Can occur in squall lines and supercells (see page 49).

HAZARDS Strong winds and lightning are a hazard to buildings, and lightning can be dangerous to people, especially golfers.

LEFT: A thunderstorm over the Timor Sea, northern Australia.

LIGHTNING

DESCRIPTION Lightning is an electrical discharge that appears as a bright flash. It makes the rumbling sound of thunder. It can occur between or within clouds and from cloud to ground (see page 50).

FORMATION Large differences in electric charge build up in a cumulonimbus cloud, which discharge as gigantic "sparks."

RANGE Worldwide, but widespread in the tropics and mid-latitudes.

SEASON Wet season in the tropics and spring and summer in mid-latitudes.

VARIATIONS Forked (streak), sheet, and chain (bead) lightning (see page 50).

HAZARDS People or animals struck by lightning can be injured or even killed. Lightning can also ignite wildfires.

RECORDS The Empire State Building in New York was once struck 15 times in 15 minutes.

LEFT: Lightning over Tucson, Arizona.

TORNADOES){

DESCRIPTION A tornado is a grayish funnel, usually about 450 feet (135 m) across, dangling from the base of a thunderstorm. It may move slowly or at up to 60 miles per hour (100 km/h).
FORMATION It's produced by severe thunderstorms when a funnel descends from the cloud, or develops near the surface and extends upward (see page 62).
RANGE Mainly in mid-latitudes.
SEASON Spring and summer.
VARIATIONS Classified by strength (see page 63), with F5 being the most severe.
HAZARDS Wind speeds up to 300 miles per hour (500 km/h) destroy any structure in the tornado's path.
RECORDS The longest path ever taken by a tornado was a 293-mile (471 km) rampage on May 26, 1917, stretching from Matoon, Illinois, to Charleston, Indiana.

RIGHT: A tornado near Laverne, Oklahoma.

WATERSPOUTS){

DESCRIPTION These are like tornadoes over water (see above), but are generally much less intense and usually not associated with thunderstorms. They may produce a plume of spray where the base touches the water.
FORMATION Waterspouts form when winds rotating near the surface interact with the updraft of a cumulus cloud.
RANGE Generally tropical and subtropical coastal waters.
SEASON Vary widely around the world.
VARIATIONS Wind speeds vary from light to about 100 miles per hour (160 km/h).
HAZARDS Stronger waterspouts pose a hazard to small boats.
RECORDS The tallest measured waterspout occurred off the coast of New South Wales, Australia, on May 16, 1898; it was 5,014 feet (1,528 m) tall.

RIGHT: A waterspout off the Costa Brava, Spain.

HURRICANES

DESCRIPTION Hurricanes are vast, tropical weather systems that rotate counter-clockwise in the Northern Hemisphere and clockwise in the south (see page 66).
FORMATION They start as large clusters of thunderstorms near the Equator and move toward subtropical areas. The Coriolis effect (see page 24) causes them to start spinning.
RANGE From about 6 to 30°N and S of the Equator to the subtropics.
SEASON Mainly in tropical wet seasons.
VARIATIONS Also known as typhoons and tropical cyclones.
HAZARDS The most severe can produce wind gusts in excess of 180 miles per hour (290 km/h), destroying most structures.
RECORDS The damage bill for Hurricane Andrew, which killed 23 people in the United States in 1992, was $25 billion.

LEFT: Damage wrought by Hurricane Andrew.

DUST DEVILS

DESCRIPTION These are a type of whirlwind that carry aloft dust particles and ground debris. They're not usually associated with any cloud formation but occur haphazardly without any obvious cause.
FORMATION They generally occur over hot ground, particularly in the desert, when strong heating of the ground causes air to rise vigorously. Wind variations over local terrain cause dust devils to rotate.
RANGE Mainly over desert areas.
SEASON Mainly in summer.
VARIATIONS Vary from very small to several feet across, and from about 100 to 3,000 feet (30 to 900 m) tall. Also known as willy-willies, dancing devils, satans, desert devils, and sand devils.
HAZARDS Strong dust devils may cause minor damage to buildings.

LEFT: Dust devils in Western Australia.

MICROBURSTS

DESCRIPTION A microburst is a cold column of air descending from a thunderstorm or large cumulus cloud. It spreads out in all directions when it reaches the ground, sometimes producing a rotating plume at the base. The dark color is due to rain in the cloud. Dust is sometimes raised by the rapidly spreading surface air.
FORMATION They form when cold downdrafts from large convective clouds hit the ground and spread outward.
RANGE In mid-latitudes.
SEASON Mainly spring and summer.
VARIATIONS Wet microbursts occur when rain reaches the ground; dry ones occur when it does not.
HAZARDS Extremely dangerous to aviation and have been responsible for several aircraft accidents.

RIGHT: A wet microburst over the Timor Sea, off the coast of northern Australia.

DUST STORMS

DESCRIPTION Fast-moving walls of dust or sand that may extend from the surface to as high as 10,000 feet (3,000 m), and extend for many miles across the ground.
FORMATION Most significant dust storms are produced by drought, which creates large areas of dry surface dust. Strong winds moving across these areas pick up this dust and carry it aloft.
RANGE Mainly desert areas, but can form in any drought-affected area.
SEASON All year but mainly in summer.
VARIATIONS Vary considerably in height and extent.
HAZARDS Pose a hazard to transportation, particularly aviation, as they reduce visibility severely. Choking clouds of dust cause great discomfort to people.

RIGHT: A dust storm in Syria.

RAINBOWS

LEFT: A rainbow in Central Australia.

DESCRIPTION Magnificent arches of colors across the sky, ranging from red, on the outside, through orange, yellow, green, blue, indigo, and violet, on the inside. The higher the sun, the flatter the arc of the rainbow; its greatest arc is when the sun is near the horizon.

FORMATION There must be sun and rain at the same time for a rainbow to form. Raindrops act as prisms to break up light into the colors of the spectrum (see page 56). To see a rainbow, you must be between the sun and the rain.

RANGE Widespread around the world.

SEASON All year.

VARIATIONS Double rainbows have two arches, with the order of colors reversed in the secondary arch. From airplanes, 360° rainbows can be seen.

CORONAS

LEFT: A double corona around the sun.

DESCRIPTION Coronas are luminous rings of light around the sun or moon. They're tinted with the colors of the spectrum, with red on the outside and violet inside. They're sometimes associated with a frontal system (see page 26).

FORMATION They're formed by light being diffracted, or bent, or as it passes through a thin layer of water droplets, often produced by altostratus or alto-cumulus clouds (see pages 86 and 87).

RANGE Usually in mid- or high latitudes.

SEASON All year.

VARIATIONS If the water droplets are not all about the same size, the coronas are deformed and the colors tend smear and lose their sharpness. Several distinct rings may be visible, becoming progressively fainter away from the center.

IRIDESCENCE

DESCRIPTION This occurs when patches of mid-level clouds such as altostratus (see page 86) are tinted with the colors of the spectrum. It can be produced by either sun- or moonlight, with the sun producing stronger colors. It's sometimes associated with a frontal system (see page 26).

FORMATION Iridescence occurs when light is diffracted, or bent, by water droplets, often produced by altostratus clouds. It forms when cloud droplets are too small for a corona to form or if the sun or moon is not directly behind the cloud (as it is with coronas).

RANGE Worldwide but rare.

SEASON All year.

VARIATIONS The shape and pattern can vary considerably.

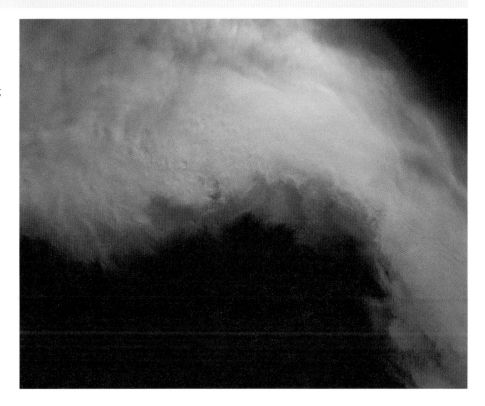

RIGHT: Iridescence on altostratus cloud.

HALOES

DESCRIPTION Haloes are white or faintly colored rings encircling the sun or moon. When colors are visible, they appear in the reverse order of those in coronas (see facing page), with red nearest the center and blue on the outside. They're sometimes associated with a cold front.

FORMATION White haloes are formed when light is refracted by ice crystals, which are usually associated with thin, high-level cloud such as cirrostratus (see page 89).

RANGE Worldwide, but more common in high latitudes.

SEASON All year.

VARIATIONS Can vary in size considerably and may be incomplete, forming an arc rather than a ring.

RIGHT: A halo around the sun.

SUNDOGS

DESCRIPTION Sundogs are two bright spots either side of the sun, creating the illusion of three suns. They're often part of a more general halo (see page 97) and are sometimes associated with an approaching frontal system (see page 26).

FORMATION They form when light is refracted, or bent, by ice crystals in cirrus clouds (see page 88). Unlike in haloes, where ice crystals are positioned horizontally in the cloud, the ice crystals must be aligned vertically for sundogs to form.

RANGE Widespread but rare.

SEASON All year.

VARIATIONS Also known as mock suns or parhelia. Can also be generated by moonlight (when they are called moondogs), but this is very rare.

LEFT: Sundogs in the Arctic.

AURORAS

DESCRIPTION Auroras look like luminous curtains of multicolored light shifting across the night sky.

FORMATION They form when charged solar particles collide with gas molecules in the earth's atmosphere. This produces bursts of visible light.

RANGE Usually in high latitudes, but can occasionally appear in lower latitudes.

SEASON Occur most frequently in an 11-year cycle, which corresponds with maximum particle emissions from the sun.

VARIATIONS Known as the aurora borealis in the Northern Hemisphere and the aurora australis in the south.

HAZARDS Can disrupt radio communications with static.

RECORDS The borealis has occurred as far south as Mexico City, and the australis has been seen as far north as Brisbane, Australia.

LEFT: The aurora borealis over Wisconsin.

GREEN FLASH

DESCRIPTION This effect is visible either just as the sun sets or as it rises. For a brief moment a green light appears just above the sun, sometimes as a brilliant emerald-green flash. It's visible only when most of the sun is below the horizon.

FORMATION The flash is caused by light being refracted, or bent, and scattered by dust particles in the atmosphere. This creates a vertical spectrum of colors, which disappear one by one below the horizon.

RANGE Worldwide but best seen at high latitudes over flat horizons, such as over the ocean.

SEASON All year.

VARIATIONS Intensity varies according to visibility.

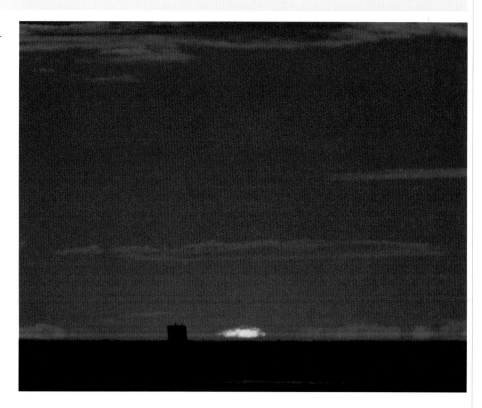

RIGHT: A green flash at sunset.

MIRAGES

DESCRIPTION Mirages are false images, or floating reflections of objects, near the horizon. They create the illusion of water on the ground in deserts, for example, where there is only hot and barren terrain.

FORMATION Mirages form when light is refracted, or bent, as it passes through layers of air of different densities. This can occur when air near the ground is heated strongly, as in deserts, or when a cold layer of air near the surface is overlaid by a warmer layer, such as over oceans.

RANGE Common over desert areas; sometimes occur over oceans.

SEASON Mainly summer over land; all year over oceans.

VARIATIONS Vary widely.

HAZARDS Can produce disorientating optical illusions.

RIGHT: A mirage in the desert, Namibia.

WORLD CLIMATIC ZONES

The earth has many different climatic zones, ranging from the icy beauty of the polar regions to the dry heat of the deserts, and from the lush tropical rain forests to the breathtaking splendor of the mountains.

ARID AND SEMI-ARID ZONES

The arid and semi-arid climatic zones are areas where rainfall is low, evaporation is high, and humidity is low. Although summer days are usually warm to hot, nights can be cold, particularly in winter when the temperature may drop below freezing.

These zones cover about one-third of the earth's land surface. The most arid parts of the globe, the deserts, have annual rainfall that is often much less than 10 inches (250 mm) and sometimes as low as 1–2 inches (25–50 mm); semi-arid regions have annual rains up to 20 inches (500 mm).

DESERTS OF THE WORLD

Arid and semi-arid zones lie mostly in sub-tropical latitudes where the semipermanent belts of high pressure are found (see page 22). Sinking air prevents clouds forming and dries and heats the atmosphere, which results in clear skies on most days.

The main subtropical arid zones in the Northern Hemisphere are the Sahara, Arabian, and Thar deserts; and the deserts of the south-western United States and Mexico. In the Southern Hemisphere the major subtropical deserts are the Kalahari and Namib deserts of Africa, the Atacama Desert in South America, and the Central Australian deserts.

Arid zones are also found in latitudes beyond the subtropics where the surrounding terrain blocks out moist, rain-bearing winds, or where the desert is well inland. The Gobi Desert of Central Asia owes its existence to both factors. The Patagonia Desert of Argentina lies in the rain shadow of the Andes.

LIFE IN THE DESERT

Only about 25 percent of the world's deserts are composed of sand; most deserts are rocky, rugged landscapes. Sand dunes cover less than a quarter of the world's largest desert, the Sahara. It extends over 3½ million square miles (9 million sq. km), an area almost as large as the United States.

Many people think that deserts are devoid of life, but they are often teeming with plants and animals that have adapted to survive the harsh, dry environment. Plants are either

ephemerals or xerophytes. Ephemerals have an annual lifecycle; they lie dormant until there is a fall of rain and then blossom into life. After a good rain flowering plants and grasses carpet the desert with color as far as the eye can see. But these colorful beauties are short-lived: when the rains have gone, they die and their seeds lie dormant again, waiting months or even years for the next good rain.

ABOVE: A Bedouin man leads his camel across the Sahara Desert, North Africa. Camels have adapted well to living in the heat. For example, they store fat in their humps, and because there is no insulation between flesh and skin, their bodies cool rapidly.

ABOVE: The arid zones of the American Southwest feature some dramatic-looking landforms, such as these buttes in Monument Valley, Arizona.

RIGHT: The starfish flower is a succulent that is native to the arid and semi-arid regions of Mozambique and southern Africa. Succulents have thick, fleshy tissues for storing water.

FAR RIGHT: Zebras that inhabit the arid regions of Namibia, such as this pair in the Namib Desert, in southwest Africa, can smell water underground. They dig a deep hole with their hooves to reach the water pools.

Xerophytes are plants that have developed ways to store and conserve the moisture they need, such as thick, fleshy leaves or trunks, extensive roots, and reduced leaf surfaces. Cacti have adapted well to survival in a desert climate: they have a tissue structure that expands to maximize water storage.

Semi-arid zones usually receive enough rain to support grassland vegetation, but rainfall is unreliable in these areas and droughts are common. Even when there is good rainfall, wildfires often ravage the resulting vegetation.

Semi-arid grasslands are found on every continent except Antarctica. They include the western prairie of North America, the steppe in southern Russia, the pampas in South America, the veldt in Africa, and the open grasslands of Australia.

Mountain Zones

Mountains experience a greater variation in weather than the lowlands, and there is much truth in the saying, "Mountains make their own weather."

Life in the Mountains

Mountain climates change with altitude, and so, therefore, does the vegetation. At low levels in many regions trees are broadleaf and deciduous (that is, they lose their leaves in fall), but these give way to conifers (mostly evergreen, needle-leaved trees) at higher, colder elevations. Farther up the mountain is the timberline: it's too cold for trees to grow above this level, and vegetation is alpine tundra, similar to the tundra of the polar zones (see page 110).

If the mountain is high enough, there may be a snow line, above which there is a permanent covering of snow or glacial ice. On mountains near the Equator the snow line is at an altitude of about 16,400 feet (5,000 m), but at the Poles permanent snow or ice occurs at ground level.

There are many animals that are native to the mountains of the world. Among the larger species are the snow leopard of the Central Asian highlands and the wapiti of western North America. The wapiti migrates to lower slopes when food becomes scarce in winter; the snow leopard hunts at altitudes up to 19,700 feet (6,000 m).

Smaller animals that inhabit the mountains include the pika of Asia and North America, and the colpeo fox of the South American Andes. The American pika doesn't hibernate but makes caches of hay in summer that sustain

it when food is scarce during winter. The colpeo fox is known to hunt to an altitude of 16,400 feet (5,000 m).

Birdlife in the mountains ranges from the tiny hummingbirds of the Andes to the California and Andean condors, which have wingspans of almost 10 feet (3 m). These mighty birds are endangered, the California condor more so than its Andean relative.

Mountain Weather

A mountain in the path of the wind inhibits the wind's free flow. Air is diverted up and over the top of the mountain or sideways around it. In both cases the wind speeds up, either because of convergence (see page 41) of the winds at the top of the mountain, or because the wind is funneled around the mountain.

Mountains can cause clouds to form (see page 40), which may lead to rain falling. If the mountain is particularly high, or if the air is very cold, snow rather than rain results.

The combination of low temperatures and strong winds on mountains means people lose more body heat than they would at the same temperature in calm conditions. This effect is known as the wind-chill factor. For this reason it's important for mountain climbers and trekkers to be well prepared before starting out. Even if it's sunny at the start, mountain weather can change for the worse very quickly.

LEFT: Tundra appears above the timberline, the area where it's too cold for trees or shrubs to grow. Here patches of lichen are scattered over the rocky landscape in Denali National Park, Alaska.

ABOVE: The Andean condor is the largest living raptor. It roosts in South American mountains, from Venezuela to Patagonia, and feeds mostly on carrion.

RIGHT: The windward side of mountains in temperate zones is usually forested because of the abundant rainfall. These firs are growing on the slopes near Mount Rainier, Washington. INSET: Like many plants of cooler regions, mountain avens grows close to the ground, where it gains warmth from the soil and protection from winds.

LEFT: The snow leopard inhabits the mountains of Central Asia. Its strong chest muscles and large forepaws help it negotiate the rugged, mountainous terrain.

TROPICAL AND SUBTROPICAL ZONES

Tropical and subtropical zones are characterized by high temperatures and humidity, and are also home to many of the world's great rain forests. The tropical zone lies between the Tropics of Cancer and Capricorn (at 23.5°N and S). The subtropical zone extends between the tropics and latitudes 30° to 40°N and S.

THE RAINY TROPICS

Broadly speaking, the tropical zone can be divided into the rainy tropics and the tropical savanna. The rainy tropics, which lie mostly within 5°–10° latitude of the Equator, and up to 20° latitude in Central America and parts of Southeast Asia, are warm, wet, and humid throughout the year. Temperatures during the day typically range from 71°F to 89°F (22°C to 32°C), and afternoon showers or thunderstorms are the norm over land.

Annual rainfall greater than 78 inches (2,000 mm) is common. At some locations, such as Monrovia, in Liberia, the annual rainfall may exceed 156 inches (4,000 mm). Vegetation is lush, and it's in the rainy tropics of Africa, South America, and Southeast Asia that the world's tropical rain forests, or jungles, are found. These forests are extremely dense, and very little sunlight penetrates the forest canopy to the ground below.

Many larger rain-forest animals live above ground in the tree canopy, and mammals that inhabit the forest floor tend to be quite small. The smallest known antelope, the king of

hares, for instance, stands only 12 inches (30 cm) high; it inhabits the tropical forests of Ghana. Insects living in rain forests, on the other hand, thrive on the high temperatures and humidity, and tend to be very large: the largest butterfly in the world, Queen Alexandra's birdwing of the rain forests of Papua New Guinea, has a wingspan of 11 inches (28 cm); the giant centipede of the Borneo jungles grows up to 10½ inches (27 cm) long.

THE TROPICAL SAVANNA

Farther away from the Equator the climate displays a distinct wet and dry season. This region is known as the tropical savanna. The wet season is accompanied by very warm, humid conditions and widespread rain, mostly from showers and thunderstorms that can continue intermittently for days at a time. The dry season is, by comparison, somewhat cooler and has almost no rain.

The Indian subcontinent has a wet and dry tropical climate. The rains that fall in the wet season are known as the Indian, or southwestern, monsoon (see pages 70–1). Other regions of the world that have a wet and dry climate are northern Australia, extensive areas in Africa and Central and South America, as well as parts of Southeast Asia.

ABOVE: *Grant's gazelles inhabit the African tropical savanna. In times of drought, when food and water become scarce, these gazelles can modify their diet by feeding at night on hygroscopic plants—that is, plants that absorb moisture from the air.*

RIGHT: *The eyelash viper is a tropical, tree-dwelling snake of Central and South American forests. Its name refers to a patch of rough scales above each eye. It preys on lizards and other small animals in the tree canopy.*

LEFT: *The green, or common, iguana inhabits tropical forests in South America. It lays its eggs in holes made in the base of trees. Hatchlings and juveniles often leave the nest together, a strategy of safety in numbers against potential predators.*

ABOVE: *Rain-forest peoples all over the world use body decoration. This man is from the Sepik River area, Papua New Guinea.*

Annual rainfall in the tropical savanna can be as much as 59–78 inches (1,500–2,000 mm), and the wet season lasts six months or so. The vegetation is open grassland with scattered clumps of trees, known as savanna woodlands. These lands are inhabited by grazing animals, such as gazelles and zebras in Africa, and kangaroos in Australia.

LIFE IN THE SUBTROPICS

Much of the subtropical zone has an arid or semi-arid climate (see page 102), but there are some parts that have either a moist climate with rain in all seasons, or a wet winter and a mostly dry summer.

Rain occurs in all seasons on the eastern side of continents within the subtropics, such as the United States and Australia. Wet winters and dry summers, which are typical of the countries bordering the Mediterranean Sea, are found on parts of the California coast near San Francisco, in the United States; the coast of central Chile; the southwest Cape Province in South Africa; and parts of the southern and southwestern coast of Australia.

Although the subtropics enjoy mostly settled weather, they do sometimes experience extremes, ranging from severe thunderstorms with flooding rains and tornadoes, to short bursts of very cold weather from the Poles.

TEMPERATE AND SUBARCTIC ZONES

Temperate zones are found in the mid-latitudes: the area between the subtropics and the Arctic and Antarctic circles (66.5°N and S). There are four distinct seasons—spring, summer, fall, and winter—in these zones. Because of the seasonal changes, food for birds and animals becomes scarce during the colder months. Some animal species, such as turtles, snakes, and frogs, simply hibernate until the warm weather returns; others, such as many species of birds, migrate to warmer regions.

In the Southern Hemisphere the largest parts of the temperate zones are oceans, but in the Northern Hemisphere the largest parts of the temperate zones are landmasses. Siberia and much of Canada are in the northern temperate zone, or subarctic. South of this zone the climate is either temperate rainy in areas exposed to the warming effects of the oceans, or more prone to extremes of heat and cold in continental areas well inland.

TEMPERATE RAINY CLIMATES

The temperate rainy zone in the Northern Hemisphere includes northwestern Europe and the Pacific Northwest Coast of North America. In the Southern Hemisphere southern Chile, the southernmost states of Australia, and the South Island of New Zealand have temperate rainy climates.

Temperate rainy climates usually have cool rather than cold winters and mild to warm summers. Although most of the precipitation that falls is rain rather than snow, and the winter is cool rather than cold, occasional intrusions of polar air do bring cold conditions and even snow to these regions.

TOP: *Fields of rapeseed in France create a vibrant patch-work of color. Farming is now the norm on land where tem-perate forests once thrived.*

ABOVE: *European otters inhabit temperate zones, but they are a rare sight in the wild. They spend much of the time in water. A layer of underfur traps air and keeps the otter's skin dry.*

LEFT: *Most of the world's wheat is grown in temperate zones. These wheat fields in Washington lie within the temperate zone on the West Coast of North America.*

The dominant natural vegetation of temperate rainy climates is forest. Much of the great forests have been cleared for agriculture, but evidence of their past grandeur can be found in the towering coastal redwoods and Douglas firs of the West Coast of the United States.

COLD CONTINENTAL CLIMATES

In Eastern Europe, East Asia, the Northeastern United States, and the subarctic the climate is cold continental. These areas are isolated from the warming effects of ocean waters, and thus undergo very harsh winters with prolonged cold, snow, and frost. On the southern fringes of this zone snow covers the ground only occasionally, but regions on the northern limits have snow cover throughout winter.

Summers in these climates are mild to warm, and there is a large annual range in temperature. For example, Chicago, in the United States, has an average summertime maximum temperature of 81°F (27°C), while the winter average minimum is 18°F (−8°C). In the subarctic the range is even greater. For instance, Irkutsk, in Siberia, has an average maximum temperature of 70°F (21°C) and an average minimum of minus 15°F (−26°C).

The main vegetation type in cold continental climates is forest. Much of it is deciduous, and it provides a flamboyant display of brilliant hues in fall. In the subarctic zone, however, extensive forests of evergreen trees—including pines, spruce, and firs—dominate the landscape. Known as the boreal forests, they are almost continuous across the continents from 50° to 60°N in the east to 60° to 70°N in the west. They are able to grow farther north in the west because these regions receive more rainfall, thanks to the westerly ocean winds, which carry moisture.

POLAR ZONES

The polar zones are the coldest and most inhospitable regions on earth, yet these sparsely populated lands possess a natural beauty that is often breathtaking.

ICY REALMS

Most of the Arctic zone, in the Northern Hemisphere, lies within the Arctic Circle at 66.5°N. It includes the Arctic Ocean, which is centered on the North Pole, as well as Greenland and the tundra of the high latitudes (the northern fringes of North America and Eurasia). The Antarctic is the vast, ice-covered continent that straddles the South Pole and lies mostly within the Antarctic Circle at 66.5°S.

The polar area of the Arctic Ocean is covered by permanent sea ice, which on average is about 11½ feet (3.5 m) thick; Greenland and Antarctica are covered by ice caps that are 1 to 2 miles (2 to 3 km) thick. Together, these ice caps account for nearly all the world's permanent ice.

Icebergs can be a hazard to shipping in polar waters. The largest are the tabular icebergs of the Antarctic, which stand some 165 feet (50 m) above the sea surface and are often more than 3,280 feet (1 km) long. Their size is truly awesome when you consider that only an eighth of the bergs appears above the surface. Some icebergs are truly gigantic. The largest tabular iceberg ever recorded was sighted off the South Shetland Islands, just off the coast of the Antarctic peninsula, in 1927. It was estimated to be 100 miles (160 km) long.

In lands inside the Arctic and Antarctic circles there are extended periods of continuous daylight in summer (known as the midnight sun) and continuous darkness in winter. At the Poles these "days" and "nights" last six months.

POLAR PLANTS AND ANIMALS

Vegetation in the Arctic is limited to the tundra: a flat, treeless plain with a cover of dwarf shrubs, mosses, and lichens. Tundra occurs on coastal Greenland and on the northern fringes of North America and Eurasia, where conditions become too cold for the great boreal forests of the Northern Hemisphere to grow. Beneath the topsoil,

LEFT: Arctic foxes are well adapted to Arctic conditions. They are excellent hunters, and their coat turns white in winter for camouflage against the snow.

BELOW: Icebergs form when great chunks of ice break away from ice shelves or glaciers. Tabular icebergs, such as this one, are the most common berg in the Antarctic.

ABOVE: An Inuit (Eskimo) hunter from Pond Inlct, Baffin Island, in Canada. Inuit people live in northern Alaska, the Canadian Arctic, and on the Greenland coast. They rely heavily on caribou, walrus, and seal for food in winter.

RIGHT: South Georgia Island, one of the subantarctic islands, is home to this king-penguin colony. Penguins have adapted well to the cold conditions: their plumage consists of a downy inner layer of feathers and a smooth, waterproof outer layer, which keeps them warm and dry.

RIGHT: The polar bear's thick coat of fur, which extends even to the soles of its feet, insulates it from the harsh cold of the Arctic winter. These solitary animals range from coastal tundra to inshore ice.

which thaws only in summer, the soil is permanently frozen (known as permafrost) to depths of tens of feet. When the topsoil thaws in the brief summer, it becomes a marshy swamp where gnats and mosquitoes and migrating birds that feed on them thrive.

The Antarctic climate is too cold to support most plant life, although lichens and mosses do manage to gain a foothold here and there. The very short Antarctic hairgrass and Antarctic pearlwort are found on the Antarctic peninsula and on nearby subantarctic islands.

In Arctic North America the tundra supports large herds of caribou. Like the closely related reindeer of Arctic Eurasia, these animals provide food and material for clothing and shelter for the many peoples who inhabit Arctic polar regions, such as the Inuit.

The Arctic is a haven for several other large mammals, too, including polar bears and musk oxen. Well adapted to survive the harsh polar winter, these animals develop thick fur and a copious layer of fat to keep them warm.

Antarctic waters offer a rich diet of fish and other sea creatures for the many species of seals and birds that breed there, including albatrosses, smaller petrels, and penguins. The largest bird of the Antarctic, the emperor penguin, stands more than 40 inches (100 cm) tall.

FORECASTING
THE WEATHER

FORECASTING HAS COME A LONG WAY SINCE
THE DAYS OF SUPERSTITION AND SKY GODS.
TODAY MAKING A FORECAST IS MUCH LIKE
ASSEMBLING A GIANT JIGSAW PUZZLE, WITH
THE PIECES BEING OBSERVATIONS, SATELLITE
PHOTOGRAPHS, RADAR, AND COMPUTER
SIMULATIONS. AS FORECASTS BECOME MORE
ACCURATE, RELIABLE PREDICTIONS UP TO A
WEEK AHEAD WILL BECOME ROUTINE.

NATURAL SIGNS

Throughout history people have looked to nature for clues to help them predict the weather. Over the centuries a weather folklore evolved that attempted to relate the appearance of the sky, as well as the behavior of plants and animals, to the weather. This folklore was often in the form of verse, or doggerel, which was easy to remember and was passed from one generation to the next.

The leaders in this area were sailors and farmers, whose safety and well-being were intimately bound up with the weather. For this reason much of this folklore has a nautical or rural flavor, such as:

Red sky in the morning, sailors take warning,
Red sky at night, sailors' delight; and
When asses their ears do toss and sway,
Rain before the end of the day.

Many of these sayings have been passed down over the centuries, and although there is some truth in a number of them, there are so many exceptions that weather folklore has not contributed a great deal to the advancement of weather forecasting.

RAINY-DAY INSECTS

The behavior of some plants and animals is considered to be the best natural predictor of weather. There is no doubt that many plants and animals are extremely sensitive to changes in temperature, humidity, air pressure, and wind speed and direction. Whether or not they are merely reacting to current conditions

LEFT: In North America the early arrival of the cedar waxwing in fall is thought to be a sign of a harsh winter. It's probably more an indication of the weather the birds have left behind, though, than any real sign of the weather to come.

or, more significantly, adapting to approaching weather is not clear, although many modern-day farmers are convinced that such natural clues are useful.

One widely known and believed natural weather clue is provided by ants. When rain is on the way some species of ants will raise the level of earth around the entrance hole to their nest, presumably to stop water running down into the nest. Some people even claim the

BELOW: Some people believe the changes in air pressure and humidity that occur ahead of storms can trigger various behavior patterns in animals. For example, bees return to their hive, left, while cows sit down, right, to keep a patch of grass dry before the rain comes.

amount of rain on the way can be estimated by the height of the barrier the ants build.

Birds flying higher than usual is believed by some to be a sign that a thunderstorm is on the way. The reason for this is that thunderstorms are triggered by strong updrafts of air, which transport low-flying insects aloft, forcing the birds to fly higher than normal in search of insects to feed on.

TALES OF FISH AND GROUNDHOGS

Some Pacific Island peoples forecast a hurricane when the usually abundant reef fish vanish. The Islanders believe these fish take shelter in rock cavities when the ocean is disturbed by a hurricane's approach.

In several places, such as England, Australia, and some Scandinavian countries, the sight of cows sitting down or huddling together during the day is a traditional sign of rain on the way.

It's believed the cows lie down to keep an area of grass dry and that they huddle together to keep warm.

According to a popular North American legend, if the groundhog, or woodchuck, emerges from its burrow on February 2 and sees its shadow (that is, the sun's shining), the next six weeks will be cold and wintry and the groundhog will return to its hole. If, however, it's cloudy, then spring has arrived and the groundhog will remain above ground.

There seems to be little truth in this legend, which is probably related to a much older English saying about the weather on Candlemas Day, which also falls on February 2.

The world is full of natural phenomena that many people believe are good weather predictors. But today weather prediction depends on large amounts of data collected by scientific instruments and analyzed by meteorologists.

WEATHER MYTHS AROUND THE WORLD

Because of the close links between the weather and human affairs, the wish to foretell and even alter the weather has ancient roots in all societies.

WEATHER OF THE GODS

In many ancient societies the weather was explained through the actions or moods of a fabulous family of sky gods, who used the weather to reward or punish that society. In general, if the gods were pleased, good weather, favorable hunting, and ideal crop conditions would follow. If not, the consequences could be dire, with flood, storms, and disease sweeping the land—a clear indication that society was currently in divine disfavor.

Some of the early weather divinities include Ra, the sun god of ancient Egypt; Thor, the Norse god of thunder and lightning; Marduk, the Babylonian sky god; and Zeus, the Greek controller of the sky.

In many ancient societies, then, people thought that weather forecasting was a matter of maintaining good communication with the

ABOVE: Quetzalcóatl had numerous roles in Aztec society. He was the god of the wind, as well as being the god of learning and the priesthood, master of life, creator and civilizer, patron of every art, and inventor of metallurgy.

RIGHT: Thor was the Norse god of thunder and lightning. He created lightning when he threw his hammer; his chariot made the sound of thunder. Here he's shown fighting the Midgard serpent, which lived under the sea.

relevant deities through ritual, prayer, and sacrifice. In this way, they thought, they would receive divine guidance about the weather to come, sometimes in the form of dreams. The ancient Aztecs of Central America, for instance, practiced human sacrifice to please their rain god, Tláloc. And today in modern, developed countries prayer is still sometimes used in an effort to break drought or quell storms.

The early "weather forecasters" therefore usually had a religious background and were often high priests, witch doctors, or medicine men—those who had the necessary contacts with the gods to enable them to predict the weather. Their duties were far more difficult than those of the modern-day meteorologist, as they not only had to predict the weather but also modify it to suit the needs and wishes of their people. One way these early weather forecasters attempted to alter the weather during periods of drought was by directing rain dances, a ceremony that was (and still is) common in several cultures, including some Native American and Australian Aboriginal tribes. The Hopi Indians of North America performed a snake dance in dry periods in the belief that this would trigger rain. For Australian Aborigines a very important deity is the Rainbow Serpent. This great snake is associated with waterholes, rain, and thunder.

In Nigeria Yoruba priests held up a specially carved wooden stick in order to repel approaching thunderstorms. In medieval Europe people used to confront storm clouds by rattling their swords or by sending volleys of arrows

or, in later times, gunfire into the sky. Sometimes witches would be burned after a hailstorm in an attempt to appease the gods.

Ancient Chinese weather mythology explained thunderstorms through the actions of Lei Kung, the thunder god, assisted by the goddess of lightning, Tien Mu, who produced bright flashes across the sky by reflecting light from her magic mirrors.

DIVINE WINDS

Provided the gods were sympathetic, weather could also be used to rout an enemy during battle. In 1274 and 1281 the Mongol warrior Kublai Khan attempted to invade Japan using his naval armadas, only to be repulsed when hurricanes smashed his fleet. The Japanese referred to these storms as divine winds, or kamikaze, sent from above to protect Japan.

In almost every recorded society there is a collection of myths that add color and history to people's efforts to understand and even master the weather.

ABOVE: This spindle whorl (used during spinning to stop the wool from slipping from the spindle) depicts the North American thunderbird and a whale. Some Native Americans believed these great birds created thunder when they beat their wings.

RIGHT: Osiris was the chief Egyptian god of the underworld and also a fertility god. Egyptians believed he controlled the flooding of the Nile.

FORECASTING THROUGH THE AGES

The use of science to aid weather forecasting may have been first attempted by the ancient Greek scholar Aristotle (384–322 BC). Aristotle wrote a huge essay called *Meteorologica*, in which he set out to explain the weather as a result of the natural interaction of the four elements (earth, fire, air, and water). Although it contained many factual errors, *Meteorologica* was the first step on the marvelous "yellow brick road" of science, which has led us into the wizard-world of radar, satellites, and supercomputers. The modern term *meteorology* derives from the title of Aristotle's work.

FROM THE RENAISSANCE TO MODERN TIMES

The next step coincided with the Renaissance, a period of great advances in science and the arts that began in the early 15th century. With the assistance of some of the greatest intellects of the time, all of whom fitted key pieces of the weather-forecasting puzzle together, the next 300 years saw a tremendous leap forward in our understanding of the physical world.

The Italian artist, architect, and engineer—an all-round genius—Leonardo da Vinci (1452–1519) designed several meteorological instruments, including the hygrometer, which measures humidity. Italian mathematician and astronomer Galileo Galilei (1564–1642) invented the thermometer, which measures temperature, while his pupil Evangelista Torricelli (1608–47) constructed the first barometer, which measures air pressure.

French scientist and philosopher Blaise Pascal (1623–62) discovered that air pressure decreases with height and that daily changes in air pressure at any one place could be related to the weather itself. The unit of pressure now used in most countries is called the hectopascal, which was named after him.

English scientist Sir Isaac Newton (1642–1727) single-handedly revolutionized major areas of mathematics and physics and was probably the first person in history to understand the riddle of the colors of the rainbow. In one of the classic experiments of science, he passed white light through a glass prism to show how it is made up of an array, or spectrum, of colors. He explained how raindrops could be thought of as miniature prisms, splitting sunlight into the colors of the rainbow (see page 56).

Anglo-Irish scientist Robert Boyle (1627–91) furthered knowledge about the nature of air itself. He discovered a fundamental natural law, today known as Boyle's law, that describes a complex relationship between the temperature, volume, and pressure of a gas.

A vital contribution was also made by the brilliant French chemist Antoine Lavoisier (1743–94), who showed that air was a mixture of several gases, including nitrogen, oxygen, and carbon dioxide.

Important work on the physics and chemistry of the processes of water-vapor condensation and its reverse, evaporation, was performed by British scientist John Dalton (1766–1844). He discovered that the amount of water vapor needed to saturate air varies greatly with temperature (see page 20).

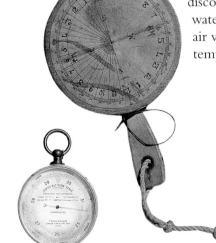

ABOVE AND RIGHT: This compass, thermometer, barometer, and sundial were used on Robert Scott's Antarctic expedition in 1910–12.

RIGHT: Each square on this French rural calendar, dating from about 1460, represents a month and depicts the task to be performed at that time of the year.

English scientist George Hadley (1686–1768) explained that global wind systems are due to the earth's rotation (see page 22). Frenchman Gustave-Gaspard Coriolis (1792–1843) demonstrated that moving objects, including winds and ocean currents, are deflected to the right in the Northern Hemisphere and to the left in the Southern Hemisphere. This phenomenon is also due to the earth's rotation and is called the Coriolis effect in his honor (see page 24).

By about the 19th century scientists had realized that weather traveled in organized "air masses," large areas of the atmosphere with similar temperature and humidity characteristics at the earth's surface (see page 26). They also noted that in mid-latitudes, such as in Europe and North America, these masses moved from west to east. They realized that if a large area of rain and strong winds were to hit the West Coast of the United States, it was

reasonable to assume that some of this stormy weather would eventually reach central and eastern North America. This, in turn, meant that if a fast communication system were devised that could send messages across large distances, meteorologists could warn people in advance of the oncoming storms.

NATIONAL WEATHER SERVICES
Such a communication system was born in 1844, when American artist and inventor Samuel Morse (1791–1872) transmitted the first telegraphic message between Baltimore,

ABOVE: Aristotle, left, was one of the earliest weather watchers. Vice-Admiral FitzRoy, right, designed a barometer.

BELOW: In 1752 Benjamin Franklin, an American philosopher and statesman, experimented with a kite attached to a wire to show that lightning was an electrical discharge.

ABOVE: This French thermometer and barometer were made in the 18th century for the Académie des Sciences, in Paris. The academy was one of several societies that undertook research on the weather.

ABOVE: This Italian food card, dating from the early 20th century, depicts a hot-air balloon on its way to the North Pole. Expeditions by balloonists revealed important information about the atmosphere.

storm-warning system, and the French meteorological service was born. By 1857 the service was receiving weather information from many parts of Europe.

Also in 1854 the British Meteorological Department was formed, and Vice-Admiral Robert FitzRoy (1805–65) became its head. FitzRoy designed a ship's barometer and started a storm-warning service for mariners.

In the United States, after storms on the Great Lakes in 1868 and 1869 sank or damaged some 3,000 ships with the loss of 530 lives, President Ulysses S. Grant ordered the formation of an army weather service, which eventually became the National Weather Service.

INTO THE MODERN ERA

The 20th century has seen staggering technological progress in weather forecasting. This was triggered by huge advances in science, including the invention of aircraft, advanced meteorological instruments, radar, and electronic computers.

The first polar-orbiting weather satellite, the United States' TIROS 1, was launched on April 1, 1960. For the first time meteorologists could photograph and study from above the great weather systems that encircle our planet.

Governments also began to recognize the importance of global cooperation in forecasting the weather. In 1961 President John F. Kennedy, of the United States, invited several different countries to participate in a project to observe the weather worldwide. The purpose was to improve weather forecasting for all nations. Although this was a time of intense rivalry between the United States and the former Soviet Union and their respective allies (known as the Cold War), some 150 countries responded positively, including the Soviet Union. As a result the World Weather Watch (WWW) was born, one of the most significant steps forward in international cooperation for weather forecasting.

Having traveled thus far on the road of science, weather prediction had now reached the gates of the fabulous city of Oz. The next few decades would see it progress at a rate undreamt of by any of the earlier weather watchers.

Maryland, and Washington, DC. This single event, more than any other, accelerated the entry of weather prediction into the scientific era. From this point on the speed of progress hit top gear and national weather services were formed in several countries.

In 1854, during the Crimean War, a disastrous storm all but wiped out the Anglo-French naval fleet when unexpected gale-force winds hit during the Battle of Balaklava. After this the Allies realized the importance of a

OBSERVING AND MONITORING THE WEATHER

When meteorologists prepare a weather forecast, the first thing they do is analyze the current state of the atmosphere. What are the temperature and air-pressure patterns at the moment? Where are the clouds and is it raining anywhere locally? To answer these questions, meteorologists use a large number of instruments to measure the various meteorological variables, which is known more formally as observing the weather.

WEATHER SATELLITES

Weather satellites are probably the single most important observational tool. There are two basic types, polar orbiting and geostationary. Polar-orbiting satellites orbit the earth at an altitude of about 550 miles (860 km) and can take reasonably detailed images of the cloud patterns below. Geostationary satellites orbit the earth at an altitude of about 22,300 miles (35,900 km) above the Equator at the same rotational speed as the earth, so they remain over the same area.

The first satellite, a polar-orbiting one, was launched in 1960. Since then dozens of these "eyes in the sky" have been launched and have revolutionized weather forecasting. Before satellites meteorologists had to try to visualize cloud patterns from the ground, which was virtually impossible in areas where clouds were widely scattered (such as over oceans). With satellites weather watchers could, for the first time, gauge the cloud extent of fronts, hurricanes, and low-pressure cells.

Modern geostationary satellites take photographs of cloud patterns at least every hour. All these images can be played back as a "movie loop," similar to time-lapse photography, which brings the atmosphere immediately to life. Weather forecasters can observe how cold fronts, hurricanes, and low-pressure cells move, enabling them to estimate their speed.

Weather satellites have become increasingly sophisticated over the years. They carry not only cameras for cloud photography but also radars and radiometers that measure cloud-top temperature and the extent of sea ice and snow cover. With instruments such as these, modern satellites monitor ocean-wave heights, sea-surface temperatures, wind speeds, and temperatures in the upper atmosphere, as well as the movements of polar sea ice.

Several nations have launched weather satellites, including the polar-orbiting satellites METEOR (Russia) and NOAA (USA), and geostationary satellites such as GOES-E and GOES-W (USA), METEOSAT (Europe), GMS (Japan), and INSAT (India).

RADAR AND WEATHER BALLOONS

Radar (which stands for radio detection and ranging) consists of a transmitter that fires off pulses of microwave radiation, a type of radiowave. If any of these pulses meet precipitation (raindrops, snowflakes, or hailstones), the pulses are reflected back to a receiver and appear on a screen. The heavier the rain, snow, or hail, the more energy is returned. Computers display this information as a colored pattern, so areas of heavy and light precipitation are visible on the screen.

LEFT: Weather balloons, filled with hydrogen or helium, are used to carry tiny instrument packages aloft. The instrument readings provide weather observers with valuable information about the upper atmosphere.

RIGHT: This computer-enhanced satellite image shows the deep spiral of cloud associated with an intense low-pressure cell. Winds from the system would be likely to exceed gale force. INSET: This image shows a tropical storm as seen from space. The three-dimensional effect is produced by clouds casting shadows. The taller clouds are thunderstorms.

Doppler radar detects in which direction the air is moving, a highly important feature for tracking such hazardous phenomena as tornadoes or microbursts (see pages 62 and 64). Two Doppler radars can be used at the same time to provide a stereoscopic view of weather systems, such as thunderstorms and squall lines.

Weather balloons, inflated with hydrogen or helium to make them lighter than air, are used to carry electronic equipment into the atmosphere. The equipment measures temperature, humidity, and air pressure as the balloon ascends, and transmits the information back to ground receiving stations. By using remote tracking techniques, such as radar, meteorologists can calculate the wind speed and direction at various heights in the atmosphere.

Automatic weather stations (AWSs) are highly technical pieces of equipment based on the ground that automatically take readings of temperature, humidity, wind speed and direction, and barometric pressure, and then transmit the information to weather services. They do this continuously and without any kind of human intervention. AWSs are designed to be sturdy and reliable in most kinds of extreme weather; some are solar powered.

INSTRUMENT SHELTERS

Some instruments are housed inside an instrument shelter, known as a Stevenson screen or weather shack. This is a box with slatted sides, elevated 4 feet (1.2 m) above the ground to allow air to circulate freely, and painted white to reflect light (see page 134). Inside is a collection of instruments: usually dry-bulb and maximum and minimum thermometers, to measure the daily temperature and its extremes, a wet-bulb thermometer, to measure humidity, and a barometer, to measure air pressure.

The main types of barometer are mercury and aneroid ones. Mercury barometers measure the height of a column of mercury in a vacuum tube; aneroid barometers measure the expansion or contraction of a vacuum cylinder.

There may also be more sophisticated instruments in the shelter such as a thermograph, which plots temperature against time,

a hygrometer, which measures humidity, and a barograph, which measures air pressure and plots the results on a graph.

Some of the instruments meteorologists use to observe the weather, such as rain gauges, anemometers, and sunshine recorders, must be exposed to the elements.

MEASURING RAIN, WIND, AND SUNSHINE

Rain gauges are the most ancient of weather-measuring instruments, and it is believed that they were used in India more than 2,000 years ago. In its simplest form the rain gauge consists

ABOVE: This temperature display unit is registering a glacial 49°F below zero (–45°C) in Fairbanks, Alaska. Such units are a convenient way to display the local temperature to the public.

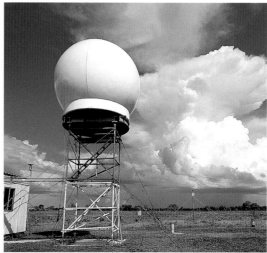

of an upright cylinder that catches any rain falling. Every 24 hours weather observers measure the rainfall in the cylinder, sometimes with a ruler. The pluviograph is a more sophisticated version of the rain gauge: it not only records how much rain has fallen but also when it fell; it also produces a graphic record of these measurements.

Anemometers are instruments for measuring the wind. The simplest example is the weather vane, a decorative device attached to the top of buildings, which has been used for many centuries to indicate wind direction. Modern anemometers are more advanced forms of the weather vane. They have rotating heads of various different types to measure the speed of the wind as well as its direction. Anemographs produce a permanent record of wind speed and direction by means of a graph on a rotating cylinder.

Being able to measure the hours of sunshine is important to farmers and for the efficiency of solar-power production. There are several complex electronic devices that can detect whether there is full sunlight or some cloud cover, but a much simpler variety consists of a giant magnifying glass in the form of a glass sphere. If there is bright sunlight, the sphere will produce a burn mark on a backing card, and as the sun moves across the sky, a profile of the cloud cover is made.

WEATHER STATIONS

Weather stations are places where observers take measurements of the atmosphere. There are many thousands of weather stations around the world that are staffed by professionals who provide data, usually every three hours, for the various national weather services. Some amateur weather observers also provide information to their local weather service. In both cases this information is taken into the global meteorological network and used to prepare forecasts across many continents up to seven days ahead.

Some people create a home station to observe the local weather as a hobby. They install instruments in their backyard and keep a day-to-day record of the weather (see page 134).

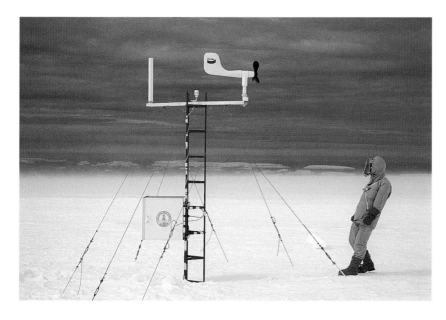

FIGURING OUT THE WEATHER

One of the most innovative developments in 20th-century weather forecasting has been the worldwide attempt to simulate, or re-create, the weather using mathematics. Meteorologists use such mathematical models to predict the movement of weather systems. These models can provide accurate forecasts up to a week ahead, as well as advance warnings about hazardous weather.

PREDICTING THE FUTURE

Many people believe that only highly trained scientists or mathematicians can understand the weather-modeling process, but this is not so. In fact, nearly all of us have used mathematics in some way to predict the future.

If, for example, we are driving down the freeway at 60 miles per hour (100 km/h) and we set the odometer at zero as we pass the town of Smithville, we know, by making a very simple mathematical calculation, that provided we keep traveling at the same speed, we will be 120 miles (200 km) beyond Smithville in two hours' time.

The process we used to arrive at this figure is similar to the processes used in mathematical weather simulation. First, we used the simple formula D = S x T, where D refers to the distance traveled, which is equal to our speed (S) multiplied by the time taken (T). This formula describes the nature of our system, which is known in mathematics as the equation of motion. In more complicated situations, such as weather forecasting, there are usually several of these equations of motion. Second, we also used a mathematical operation (in this case multiplication) which can handle, or solve, this equation. Finally, we took into account our starting conditions; that is, when we set the odometer to zero, we were traveling at 60 miles per hour (100 km/h). These are known as the initial conditions of the system.

This very simple example demonstrates the general principles of mathematical simulation; that is, we can predict the future state of a system if:

1. we know the equation(s) of motion;
2. we can solve the equation(s) by some sort of mathematical process;
3. we know the initial conditions.

In predicting the weather, however, forecasters have to use six, rather than simply one, main equations of motion. These are vastly more complicated than the equation in our simple example, and very intricate mathematical procedures are required to solve them. Because of this, meteorologists use sophisticated high-speed computers, capable of performing millions of calculations per second.

The initial conditions for weather predictions are also very difficult to determine, because they depend on thousands of individual weather observations from around the world. These observations include, among others, wind speed and direction, temperature, humidity, atmospheric pressure, and local upper-air data from balloon flights.

BELOW: A Cray X-MP/48 super-computer has enormous calculating power: it can process millions of pieces of information per second. Computers such as this one are constantly helping to improve mathematical weather simulation.

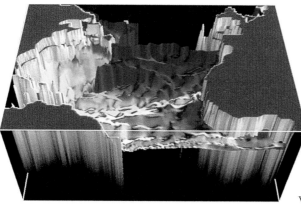

RIGHT: Meteorologists make computer simulations of ocean currents to help them understand how oceans affect weather (see page 34). This is an ocean-circulation model run by the US National Center for Atmospheric Research

SUPERCOMPUTERS AND "SUPERSTORMS"

This type of simulation proved to be invaluable in March 1993, when a "superstorm" hit part of the East Coast of the United States, leading to unprecedented heavy snowfalls over many of the eastern states. With the aid of state-of-the-art computers, the US National Weather Service was able to use mathematical modeling—along with information provided by radar, regularly updated weather maps, and satellite images—to issue accurate predictions and warnings about the severe storm 24 hours in advance.

Accurate forecasts of extreme weather not only save human lives, but also help to minimize damage to property. In dollar terms alone, the annual savings involved far outweigh the cost of providing the forecasting service.

As computers become more sophisticated and are able to quickly process greater volumes of data, and as more countries cooperate in the exchange of weather information, mathematical modeling will no doubt produce more accurate and detailed weather forecasts than are possible today. Mathematical modeling will undoubtedly remain the main instrument of weather prediction well into the 21st century.

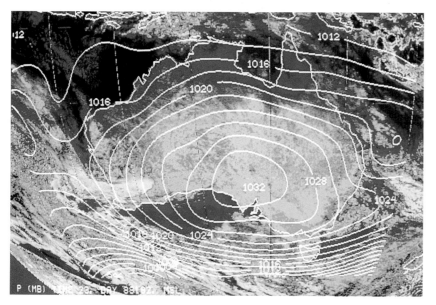

ABOVE: In this Australian system a computer-produced synoptic chart (see page 128) has been superimposed on a color-enhanced satellite photograph. The lines on the chart are isobars.

RIGHT: The "superstorm" of March 1993 produced heavy snowfalls over New York City. Computer simulations from the US National Weather Service enabled excellent forecasts to be issued well in advance of the storm's arrival.

CHARTING THE WEATHER

Charts are the main tool meteorologists use to describe the present and future state of the weather. Synoptic charts describe the current weather and prognostic charts describe the likely future weather.

MAPPING THE PRESENT

A synoptic chart presents a summary of the current weather. Although synoptic charts are taken for granted these days, they are one of the wonders of modern times. They were made possible only with the invention of high-speed, electronic communication across the world. They date from the 1840s, when Samuel Morse (see page 120) invented the telegraph—the first device to send messages by electricity. Today synoptic charts rely on information transmitted by various methods of high-speed electronic communication, collected both nationally and internationally.

A synoptic chart is the work of hundreds of people working as a team. At certain, fixed times right around the world (usually every three hours), weather observers take readings from their instruments and transmit them to collecting offices. Meteorologists also gather data from automatic weather stations (see page 124). In addition, ships at sea record details about the local weather and send the information to collecting offices.

Usually, each country concentrates mainly on its national weather, but most weather services also monitor the weather conditions in their hemisphere or across the world.

Meteorologists gather together all this information—temperature and humidity, wind speed and direction, cloud cover, and atmospheric pressure—and plot it on charts using symbols (see page 131). Because these charts are usually prepared every three hours, they are known as the 9 AM chart, the noon chart, the 3 PM chart, and so on.

The synoptic chart is, therefore, a "snapshot" of an area's weather at a particular time. Meteorologists study a synoptic chart to identify the pressure patterns. These indicate frontal systems, areas of high and low pressure, (see pages 26 and 28), and any regions with severe weather. When they compare a series of

synoptic charts, meteorologists can calculate how fast these various systems are moving, which helps them to prepare forecasts and warnings (see page 132).

MAPPING THE FUTURE

Prognostic charts look similar to synoptic charts, except that they show areas where meteorologists predict that fronts, highs, lows, and severe weather will form in the future. Prognostic charts are prepared for fixed times

ABOVE: A forecaster at work in the British Meteorological Office at Bracknell, England. Scenes such as this are common in weather offices every day around the world, as information is collected and exchanged internationally.

in the future, from a few hours up to a week in advance. Long-range forecasts (up to three months ahead) are largely based on statistics, but this is likely to change in the future.

Prognostic charts used to be prepared manually, usually by senior meteorologists who were very familiar with the weather systems in their particular area. But since the early 1970s computers and mathematical weather simulations (see page 126) have been used increasingly to prepare prognostic charts.

Meteorologists test the accuracy of these forecast charts against the information provided by synoptic charts. For instance, they might compare the prognostic chart that predicts the position of the weather patterns at 9 AM in two days' time with the 9 AM synoptic chart when it becomes available. By testing the accuracy of prognostic charts in this way, weather services can detect persistent errors or biases in the charts, and so take steps to improve their accuracy.

READING A WEATHER MAP

Weather maps, known to meteorologists as synoptic or prognostic charts (see pages 128–9), appear every day in newspapers and on television screens around the world. Since the early 1990s they have also appeared on fax databases and on the Internet.

INTERNATIONAL WEATHER SYMBOLS

Many weather phenomena are designated by an internationally recognized symbol (see box opposite). A small symbol with an internationally agreed meaning is a neat, shorthand way of communicating often quite complicated information on synoptic charts. These symbols are instantly recognized by meteorologists or professional observers around the world and are among the tools of trade for basic weather observation.

FEATURES OF WEATHER MAPS

First establish whether the map you're looking at is a prognostic chart or a synoptic chart (see page 128). This is usually indicated at the base of the map. Different weather services have different ways of presenting information on weather maps: lines of equal pressure (isobars) are a major feature on some maps, but some countries publish simpler versions that describe temperature patterns (isotherms).

Centers of high- and low-pressure systems are labeled, sometimes with the letters H and L. If isobars appear, you'll notice that the air pressure increases towards the center of a high, and decreases towards the center of a low. In most cases you'll find that the individual isobars and central pressure of the system are labeled in hectopascals (hpa), or sometimes in millibars. However, some newspaper weather maps note only the central pressure. Generally, if the central pressure of a low is less than 1,000 hectopascals, and that of a high is greater than 1,030 hectopascals, these are considered to be strong atmospheric circulations of air.

Usually wind speed and direction are shown only on synoptic charts. But it's possible to estimate the wind speed and direction on a prognostic chart. In the Northern Hemisphere air flows counterclockwise about lows and clockwise about highs, in a direction roughly

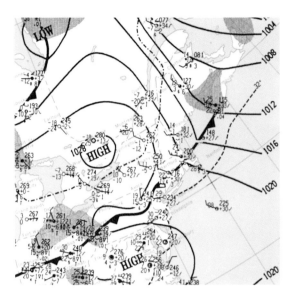

LEFT: This synoptic chart (see page 128) shows two areas of high pressure over eastern North America, with a cold frontal system (see page 26) between them. Shaded areas indicate regions where either rain or snow is falling. The solid lines are isobars, and the dashed lines are isotherms.

parallel to the isobars. The wind direction is reversed in the Southern Hemisphere. If the isobars are closely spaced over a particular area, the winds here will be stronger than over areas where the isobars are widely separated.

If the map doesn't show isobars, but only labels the centers of pressure systems, then it's still possible to estimate wind direction from these rules, although you'll have to calculate the likely wind strength from other sources. Consider the effects that terrain, as well as sea and land breezes (see page 44), have on winds.

With an estimated wind direction, it is often possible to predict future temperatures. If a prognostic chart shows a low centered over the eastern seaboard, for instance, with a central pressure less than 1,000 hectopascals, it's possible that strong, northerly winds will result over much of the eastern United States, with below-average temperatures. This is because winds flow counterclockwise around the low, producing northerly winds. These will bring air down from over Canada, resulting in colder than average temperatures for the eastern states.

Other prominent features on weather maps are cold and warm fronts (see page 26). Warm fronts are usually depicted by lines with small semicircles; cold fronts are symbolized by lines with triangles. If a prognostic chart shows the arrival of a cold or warm front, a change in the weather is likely. Look for an increase in clouds and check the barometer for falling pressure.

RIGHT: Extensive areas of valley fog float over Blue Ridge Parkway, North Carolina. INSET: A contrasting cloudmass looms over the prairie.

INTERNATIONAL WEATHER SYMBOLS

CURRENT WEATHER

ꝯ	light drizzle
ꝯ ꝯ	steady, light drizzle
ꝯ/ꝯ	intermittent, moderate drizzle
ꝯꝯ	steady, moderate drizzle
ꝯ/ꝯ	intermittent, heavy drizzle
ꝯꝯꝯ	steady, heavy drizzle
●	light rain
● ●	steady, light rain
●/●	intermittent, moderate rain
●●●	steady, moderate rain
●/●	intermittent, heavy rain
●●●	steady, heavy rain
✳	light snow
✳ ✳	steady, light snow
✳/✳	intermittent, moderate snow
✳✳	steady, moderate snow
✳/✳	intermittent, heavy snow
✳✳✳	steady, heavy snow
⍌	hail
∿⌣	freezing rain
⌠∿	smoke
)(	tornado/waterspout
⸹	dust devils
⌠⟶	dust storms
≡	fog
⎕	thunderstorm
⟨	lightning
⌀	hurricane

SKY COVERAGE

◯	no clouds
◔	one-tenth covered
◑	two- to three-tenths covered
◓	four-tenths covered
◐	half covered
◓	six-tenths covered
◕	seven- to eight-tenths covered
◑	nine-tenths covered
●	completely overcast
⊗	sky obscured

LOW-LEVEL CLOUDS

—	stratus
⌣	stratocumulus
⌢	cumulus
⌂	cumulus congestus
⌂	cumulonimbus calvus
⎈	cumulonimbus with anvil

MID-LEVEL CLOUDS

∠	altostratus
⌣	altocumulus
M	altocumulus castellanus

HIGH-LEVEL CLOUDS

⌣	cirrus
2	cirrostratus
⌇	cirrocumulus

WIND SPEED

Symbol	mph	km/h
◎	calm	calm
—	1–2	1–3
⌐	3–8	4–13
⌐	9–14	14–23
⌐	15–20	24–33
⌐	21–25	34–40
◣	55–60	89–97
◣◣	119–123	192–198

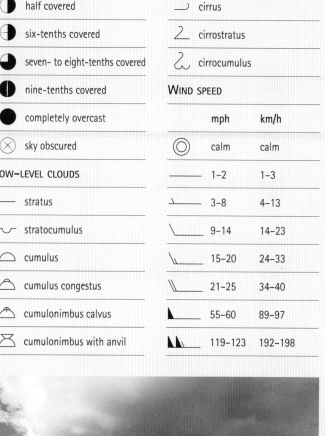

WARNINGS AND FORECASTS

Once a national weather service has prepared a weather forecast, the forecast is of no further use until it can be distributed to the people who need it. Everybody has some interest in the weather, but some people—such as farmers, aviators, and mariners—have a particular interest because it's important to their livelihood or well-being.

FAST FORECASTING: THEN AND NOW

The earlier the warning people have, the more effectively they can plan for future weather. So the faster the forecasts can be distributed, the greater their value. If rain is on the way, for instance, farmers may wish to delay irrigation, pest spraying, or harvesting. Pilots need to know if significant winds are forecast as such winds can affect aircraft landing or taking off, and flight paths may have to be altered. Strong winds may also be crucial to firefighters' success in putting out wildfires.

In the late 19th century forecasts were often sent by telegraph and displayed at public places, such as town-hall noticeboards. Strong-wind warnings were given by displaying various types of flags and pennants from prominent places. Daily newspapers also published forecasts, as they still do today. During the early decades of the 20th century forecasts were broadcast on the radio, which was, and still is, a highly effective way of reaching a large number of people quickly with the most up-to-date information.

LEFT: Weather information and reliable forecasts are vital to many industries. In drought-stricken areas, such as that seen here, farmers must make arrangements to get food and water to their animals. The more warning they have of changing conditions, the better.

By the late 1940s and 1950s many countries had a television service that broadcast weather forecasts. This was a veritable information revolution: for the first time television allowed up-to-date images of the weather, both local and global, to be transmitted directly into people's homes.

MODERN TECHNIQUES

During the 1960s satellite photographs were published in newspapers and shown on television. This was an exciting step forward in monitoring the weather, and created an ever increasing demand to see what the weather looked like from space. By stringing several such photographs together, meteorologists could make a "movie loop" that showed how

FORECASTING ON TELEVISION

Television has revolutionized the way warnings and forecasts are communicated. The presentation methods have evolved considerably over the years, progressing from static displays of isobaric charts, to highly sophisticated sequences that show satellite "movie loops." Interestingly, the weather presenters themselves often become well-known figures with a considerable public following.

Color-enhanced satellite weather pictures, far left, and well-known US presenter Willard Scott, left.

ABOVE: *A satellite image of flooding in the St Louis area in 1993, when the Mississippi and Missouri rivers burst their banks. Meteorologists use satellite photography to identify the extent of flood-waters, enabling them to predict where flooding in other areas will occur.*

ABOVE RIGHT: *A weather display unit in New York City during a snowstorm. Such units are common in major cities.*

the clouds were moving and changing over time. This, too, became essential television viewing for the weather enthusiast.

Another information revolution, almost on a scale with that of television, occurred during the 1980s and '90s with the arrival of nonmedia delivery systems, such as fax databases and the Internet. With these systems people can access weather information when they want to, rather than waiting for the radio or TV weather forecast. Access to weather information on the Internet, particularly, increased enormously during the 1990s (see page 135). Eventually, it's likely that more people will obtain weather forecasts on the Net than from media forecasts.

Perhaps the most vital function of any national weather service is issuing warnings to the public about severe weather to come. Many studies have revealed that timely warnings save human lives and help prevent damage to property. The US National Weather Service, for example, issues warnings about hurricanes,

tornadoes, severe thunderstorms, gale-force winds, and floods. It issues hurricane warnings through the media, as well as over special emergency channels, giving residents enough time to batten down their property or evacuate. Tornado warnings allow people to seek shelter, and thunderstorm warnings are an important part of aviation safety (see pages 62–6).

WEATHER ORGANIZATIONS

Most countries have their own weather services, which come under the umbrella of the World Meteorological Organization (WMO). With more than 170 member countries, the WMO coordinates weather monitoring globally and issues information through its three world meteorological centers: Washington, in the United States; Moscow, in Russia; and Melbourne, in Australia. Known as the World Weather Watch (WWW), it was initiated by President John F. Kennedy in 1961.

INSTALLING A HOME STATION

Observing the weather can be a fascinating hobby for people of all ages. By making regular observations, measurements, and recordings of the weather, you can learn about the weather patterns of your local area and gain an understanding of how the elements interact on a broader scale.

STARTING OUT

If you decide to try weather watching as a hobby, a good way to start is to install your own home weather station. What kind of station you can set up will be determined not only by how much you want to spend, but also by where you live. If you live in an apartment, for instance, and have access only to a balcony, you could install instruments that measure temperature, humidity, and barometric pressure. But it will be impossible to install a rain gauge, anemometer, or sunshine recorder properly on a balcony.

If you live several stories up, you will need to correct the pressure reading for height by adding 1 hectopascal for every 33-foot (10 m) increase in altitude. For instance, if you live about 200 feet (60 m) above sea level, and your barometer reads 1,010 hectopascals, add 6 hectopascals to correct the reading to sea level.

If you have a backyard, you may be able to install a more complete set of instruments, and you may even have space to erect an instrument shelter. There are rules for the exposure of these instruments, so check them out with your local weather-service office. It may be impossible to meet these requirements in your backyard because of nearby buildings or trees. However, even where the instruments are not in an ideal position, your readings can, over time, give you an idea about the general weather patterns in your area.

It's best to begin slowly when you're starting out: purchase only the basic instruments such as a rain gauge, dry-bulb thermometer and maximum and minimum thermometer, and an aneroid barometer. Seek advice from the local weather-service office on how and what to record from these instruments. You can also cross-check your readings with those published and broadcast by local media.

If you decide to take things further, you may like to purchase a more comprehensive selection of instruments, including a hygrometer, anemometer, and sunshine recorder (see pages 124–5).

COMPUTERS AND CAMERAS

You can set up quite an advanced home weather station with the aid of software packages that link instrument readings to your computer. Once the readings have fed into the computer, it can present the data in graph form. You can keep this for your personal weather records.

BELOW: *An instrument shelter has slatted sides to allow air to circulate freely, and is painted white to reflect light. The shelter should be erected 4 feet (1.2 m) above the ground. It normally houses a dry-bulb, wet-bulb, and maximum and minimum thermometers, together with a barometer (see page 124).*

TOP AND ABOVE: There are many types of meteorological instruments available commercially. A rain gauge, above, is one of the easiest instruments to install. A barograph, top left, measures air pressure and plots the results on a graph. Some instruments combine different functions, such as this hygrometer, thermometer, and barometer in one, top center; and barometer and dual thermometer and hygrometer, top right.

You could enhance these records by photographing weather phenomena such as interesting cloud formations, hail, heavy rain, rainbows, and haloes. The best type of camera for this is the 35 mm single lens reflex (SLR). Most SLR cameras have automatic focusing and exposure functions, enabling even beginners to take high-quality photographs in different conditions.

WEATHER ON THE NET

If you're convinced that weather watching is the hobby for you, then it's a good idea to network and link up with others who share your interest. Your national weather service will have information about local weather interest groups, and you can also get information about such groups on the Internet (see box opposite). The GLOBE program (see box opposite) is a good way for schools to become involved in worldwide weather watching.

In some cases it may be possible to become an official observer and provide readings to the national weather service. However, whether the weather service will accept you as an official observer will depend on a number of factors. These include the type of instruments you have and how they're installed; whether you can provide regular readings all year; and whether the service requires observations from your area. Happy weather watching!

WEATHER INTERNET ADDRESSES

NATIONAL AERONAUTICS AND SPACE ADMINISTRATION (NASA): satellite images of earth and atmosphere, images from the Hubble Space Telescope, and latest information about projects, shuttle missions, etc. http://www.nasa.gov/

NATIONAL CLIMATIC DATA CENTER (NCDC): climatic information for the US and the rest of the world. http://www.ncdc.noaa.gov/

NATIONAL OCEANIC AND ATMOSPHERIC ADMINISTRATION (NOAA): forecasts, satellite images, weather maps. http://www.noaa.gov/

WEATHERNET: lists nearly 300 Internet weather sites, plus maps and graphics. http://cirrus.sprl.umich.edu/wxnet/

WORLD WIDE WEB VIRTUAL LIBRARY: METEOROLOGY: international weather information and links. http://www.met.fu-berlin.de/DataSources/MetIndex.html

GLOBAL LEARNING AND OBSERVATIONS TO BENEFIT THE ENVIRONMENT (GLOBE): an international environmental research program that links schools around the world (see page 154). http://globe.fsl.noaa.gov/

THE WEATHER CHANNEL: weather for US cities. http://www.weather.com/

WEATHER UNDERGROUND INC: information on US weather. http://www.wunderground.com/

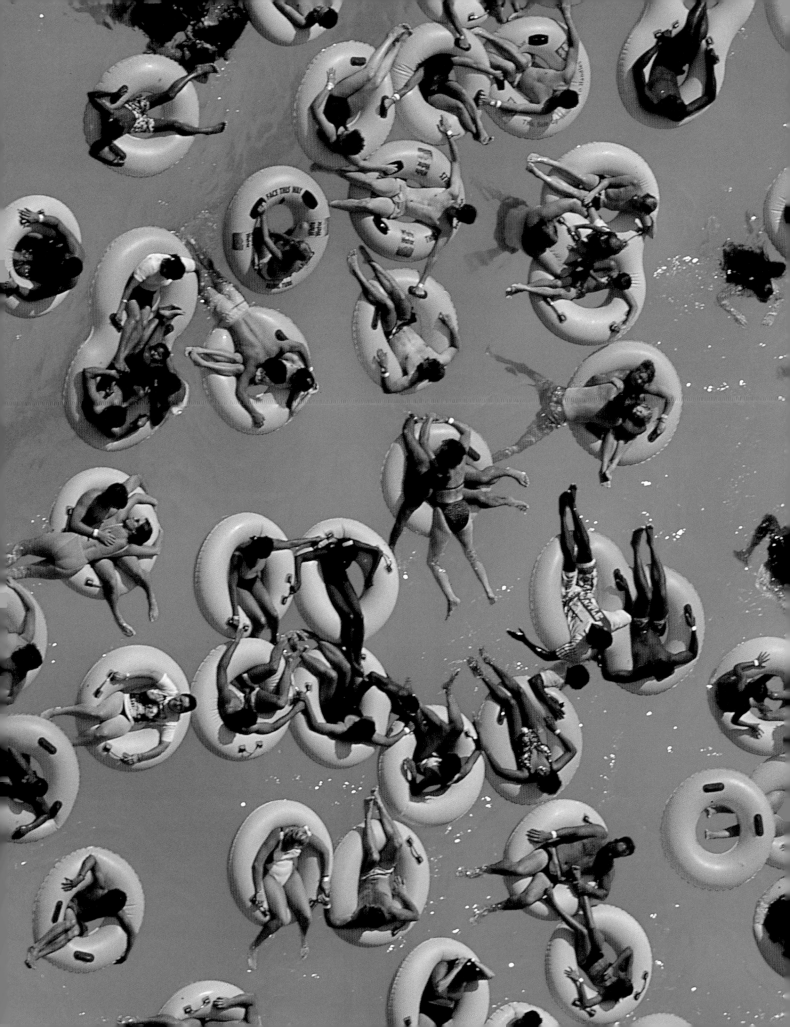

PEOPLE AND WEATHER

THE WEATHER AFFECTS EVERYTHING IN
OUR DAILY LIFE: OUR HEALTH, THE AIR
WE BREATHE, OUR ACTIVITIES, THE CLOTHES
WE WEAR. YET WHAT WE DO ALSO AFFECTS
THE WEATHER. HOW QUICKLY WE REPAIR THE
OZONE "HOLE," CONTROL ACID RAIN, AND
SLOW DOWN THE ENHANCED GREENHOUSE
EFFECT WILL INFLUENCE THE QUALITY OF LIFE
FOR GENERATIONS TO COME.

MILLIONS OF YEARS OF CLIMATE CHANGE

Climate researchers around the world are doing some intriguing detective work. They have been able to identify variations in the average temperature of the earth, which is currently about 59°F (15°C), going back more than a million years. During this period there have been several ice ages when the average global temperature plunged to 52°F (11°C), causing large parts of the world to be covered with snow and ice.

COOL TIMES, WARM TIMES

The fortunes of various civilizations have ebbed and flowed with the warm and cool spells of the past 1,000 years. The Mayan civilization of Central America showed a rapid decline between 800 and 1000 AD, and a key reason for its demise may have been repeated crop failures caused by drought. Although the most recent ice age ended about 10,000 years ago, there was a cool period between the 15th and 19th centuries when average temperatures were 2°F to 3°F (1°C to 2°C) cooler than they

LEFT: A study of Arctic and Antarctic ice sheets has provided valuable clues to the earth's climate as far back as 220,000 years ago.

BELOW: Both corals and trees exhibit growth rings that can be used to gather clues about climate change. The most useful tree rings are from the very old, slow-growing trees. These are often found in climates where the annual growth is small and occurs during a short, warm spell.

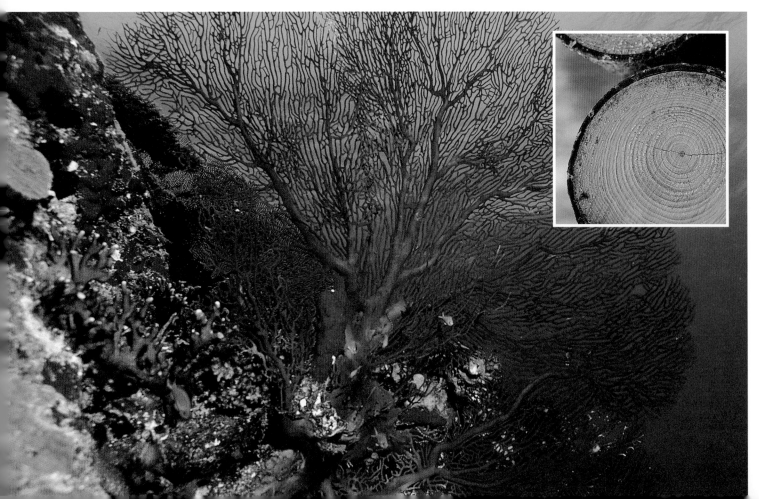

ABOVE: *Fossils, such as this fish and palm from the Green River Formation, Wyoming, have provided researchers with information on the earth's temperature trends millions of years ago.*

in the not too distant future. A major effect of past global warming was the extinction of many plant and animal species, which doesn't augur well for some of our already endangered species.

DISCOVERY OF THE PAST

Although Galileo invented the thermometer over 400 years ago in 1592 (see page 118), the earliest reliable recorded measurements of temperature date back only 300 years. And it's only during the past 100 years that temperatures have been accurately measured in enough locations to be useful for global climate studies.

One of the earliest successful techniques used to unravel the mysteries about the climates of the past was the study of tree rings. Provided a tree grows in a region where there is a distinct growing season, it will produce one ring per year. Wide rings indicate a good growing season; narrow ones indicate a poor one. Long-lived, slow-growing trees, such as the bristlecone pine tree of the mountains of California, in the United States, are the best trees for this type of investigation.

In 1904 American researcher Andrew E. Douglass was the first person to use this technique; he charted temperature trends spanning 4,000 years. A similar method has been applied to long-lived corals, which also have growth rings that can be linked to past rainfall and sea-temperature changes over several centuries.

Researchers have discovered that the thick Greenland ice sheet contains a record that goes back much further. Individual layers of snow show evidence of the variations in snowfall, temperature, and atmospheric composition for 15,000 years. The Antarctic ice sheets are older and provide an even longer record: researchers can study the ice cores to deduce general trends in climate over the last 220,000 years.

Gleaning clues about weather further back in time becomes increasingly difficult. However, using studies of ocean- and lake-bed sediments containing pollen grains and minute fossils, each requiring a certain temperature to thrive, researchers have identified broad temperature trends from a million or more years ago. Even Sherlock Holmes would be impressed!

are now. This cool period probably occurred worldwide, but most evidence relates to the Northern Hemisphere. For instance, it wasn't uncommon at this time for the River Thames, in London, to freeze over. By the 15th century the Norse colony on Greenland, established some 500 years earlier, was wiped out, probably because of the increasing cold.

The earth's highest average temperature over the past million years was about 61°F (16.5°C); it occurred most recently about 5,000 years ago. If the enhanced greenhouse effect (see page 140) is not countered, it's likely the earth will exceed this temperature toward the end of the 21st century.

The facts that scientists have pieced together about warm periods in the earth's past could provide some valuable clues to what to expect

LIFE ON EARTH: THE GREENHOUSE EFFECT

Viewed from space, the earth appears to wear a thin, blue cloak, called the atmosphere (see page 10). Without this blue cloak, life on earth would not exist.

THE BLUE PLANET

Since the 19th century scientists have known that the atmosphere, assisted by the oceans, has the crucial ability to store heat from the sun. If it were not for the atmosphere, the average temperature on earth would be 0°F (–18°C), which would be far too cold for most species to exist. Because of the atmosphere, the average temperature is a relatively warm 59°F (15°C). The atmosphere's capacity to retain heat is known as the greenhouse effect, because it's similar to the way glass in a greenhouse lets in sunlight but minimizes heat loss.

The atmosphere also moderates the difference in temperature between day and night, so we don't get extremes of heat and cold. This is particularly critical in those countries close to the Arctic and Antarctic circles, which experience very long days in summer and equally long nights in winter.

GASEOUS SUBSTANCES

There are several gases in the atmosphere that contribute to the greenhouse effect. Water vapor and carbon dioxide are the two most important greenhouse gases; methane, nitrous oxide, ozone, and (since the 1950s) synthetic chlorofluorocarbons (CFCs) play lesser roles. Although they occur only in small percentages in the atmosphere, these gases allow about half of the incoming sunlight (solar radiation) to reach the earth's surface, but restrict the outward passage of the reradiated heat into space.

CLIMATE CHANGE

Today we know that certain human activities such as burning fossil fuels—oil, coal, natural gas, and petroleum products—add to the concentration of greenhouse gases in the atmosphere and produce an "enhanced greenhouse effect." The first person to recognize the possibility of human activities changing the earth's climate was Swedish chemist Svante Arrhenius. In 1896 he calculated that if activities such as burning coal doubled the concentration of carbon dioxide in the atmosphere, the temperature of the earth would rise by 9°F to 11°F (5°C to 6°C).

If there is an increase in greenhouse gases equivalent to a doubling of carbon dioxide, the latest figures from the Intergovernmental Panel on Climate Change (IPCC), a global panel of the world's best atmospheric scientists, predict an average global temperature increase of between 3°F and 8°F (1.5°C and 4.5°C). So Arrhenius's estimate was not a bad one, considering that he made it 100 years ago.

Recent studies have shown that the average temperature of the earth has risen by up to 1°F (0.6°C) during the 20th century. This temperature rise doesn't seem very large when you consider that some daily temperatures vary by

LEFT: Trees help to absorb the extra carbon dioxide we produce in burning fossil fuels such as oil, coal, and gasoline.

ABOVE: Widespread destruction of the tropical rain forests is contributing to the increasing levels of carbon dioxide in the atmosphere. This Brazilian forest is being cleared for farmland.

tens of degrees with few apparent problems. Scientists can detect this rise only by closely studying temperature records spanning many decades from all over the globe. The significance of the rise becomes clear, however, once we compare it with temperature changes in earlier periods of the earth's history. From studying the history of the earth's climate (see page 138), we know that the average

temperature rise from an ice age to the middle of the warm period that follows is only 9°F to 11°F (5°C to 6°C). Yet the impact of ice ages on every living thing on the planet was quite dramatic. Polar climates expanded toward the Equator and changes in vegetation led to loss of habitat, so many species of plants and animals became extinct. For example, dinosaurs may have died out during such an ancient ice age.

FOSSIL FUELS AND FORESTS

Because of our great dependence on fossil fuels, it's highly likely that concentrations of greenhouse gases in the atmosphere will double toward the middle or end of the 21st century. The amount of carbon dioxide in the atmosphere has already risen by approximately 25 percent since the middle of the 19th century.

The continuing destruction of the world's great forests, especially the tropical rain forests, accelerates this build-up of carbon dioxide. Trees store carbon dioxide in their tissues as carbon compounds. When the trees are cut down and decay or are burned, the carbon is released into the atmosphere as carbon dioxide. Cultivated plants that replace the forest trees don't absorb and store as much heat-retaining carbon dioxide.

The rise in temperature caused by increasing greenhouse gases will not affect all parts of the world in the same way. Scientists believe some areas will become significantly warmer; others, such as tropical areas, wetter; and others, such as Mediterranean climates, drier. They believe the polar regions will experience greater temperature changes than elsewhere, causing permafrost (areas of frozen ground) to thaw. The extinction of many already threatened plant and animal species will follow. The paths, frequency, and intensity of major storms will possibly change, bringing severe weather, such as hurricanes and typhoons, to areas that have seldom before experienced them. Tropical

diseases such as malaria will spread. Glaciers are already in retreat, and the earth's snowfields are shrinking.

The rise in air temperature will also cause the sea level to rise: two-thirds of the rise will be due to the oceans expanding as they warm, with melting glaciers being smaller contributors. Scientists predict the rise will be some 8 inches to 3 feet (20 cm to 1 m), which will threaten the existence of the millions of people who

ABOVE: Emissions from industrial centers are a significant contributor to greenhouse gases. In 1996 scientists estimated the total global emissions of carbon dioxide to be approximately 6 billion tons (5.4 billion tonnes) of carbon from the energy sector alone.

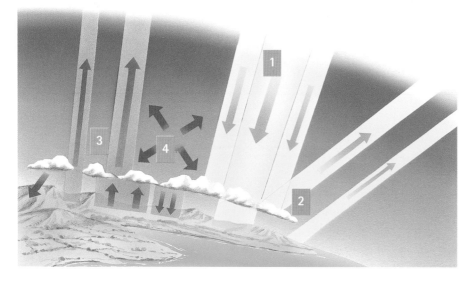

THE GREENHOUSE EFFECT

1. Of all the sunlight (solar radiation) that enters the atmosphere, only 51 percent reaches the earth's surface directly.

2. Clouds, air, and the earth's surface absorb some radiation and reflect the rest back out to space.

3. The earth, air, and clouds reradiate the absorbed energy in all directions, some out to space.

4. Some of the outgoing radiation is recaptured by greenhouse gases and clouds, and reradiated in all directions.

ABOVE: *Motor vehicles generate greenhouse gases by burning petroleum products, such as gasoline and diesel fuel. In Canada, for example, the transportation sector accounts for 49 percent of the total carbon-dioxide emissions. The construction of freeways, such as this one in Montreal, Canada, encourages more and more people to use their cars.*

live in low-lying areas. Higher sea levels would reduce the protection coastal reefs offer, causing storms to have more devastating effects. The delta areas of major rivers, such as the Ganges, in Bangladesh, and low-lying islands in the Indian and Pacific oceans are most at risk. Another concern is that even if the build-up of greenhouse gases is reversed now, the earth's climate will continue to change for several decades, and the sea level will continue to rise for the next 100 to 200 years.

DAMAGE CONTROL

Climate change on this great scale will almost certainly disrupt the delicate balance of plant and animal habitats, leading to the extinction of an increasing number of species.

The world's developed countries are starting to look at ways to reduce the enhanced greenhouse effect. Industries are beginning to use fewer and cleaner fuels and phasing out CFCs, which until recently were used in aerosols and in refrigeration and foam-plastic manufacturing. Automobile manufacturers are making their vehicles more fuel efficient. Methane, a very active greenhouse gas that leaks from refuse dumps is being harnessed and used to generate power (see page 74). This is reducing our reliance on fossil fuels.

Most important, we're all beginning to realize that we must use scarce resources wisely and consider the impact our activities are having on what is probably the only planet in the solar system sustaining life—our home!

THE OZONE LAYER

Ozone is the Jekyll and Hyde gas of the atmosphere. In high concentrations it is toxic to living things (it can damage the tissue of plants and animals), yet it is critical to all life on the planet. Ozone in the atmosphere absorbs most of the sun's biologically damaging ultraviolet B (UVB) radiation, allowing only a small amount to reach the earth's surface.

A RARE GAS
Approximately 90 percent of the earth's natural ozone is located in a layer in the stratosphere. The ozone layer, as it's commonly referred to, is between 6 and 30 miles (10 and 50 km) above sea level. Ozone is one of the rarest gases in the atmosphere: there are only 3 molecules of ozone in every 10 million molecules of air. If all the ozone directly above you were brought to the earth's surface, there would be a layer of ozone only ⅛ inch (3 mm) thick.

Much of the remaining ozone is found near the earth's surface, and a large amount is produced by human activities such as burning fossil fuels, particularly by vehicles. Ozone is a key ingredient in smog and is highly toxic, making it the target of numerous programs to control pollution caused by vehicles. This ozone tends to remain heavily concentrated around cities and, being less than 10 percent of the total ozone in the atmosphere, plays only a minor role in reducing incoming UVB radiation.

THE "HOLE" IN THE OZONE LAYER
In the 1920s British physicist Gordon Dobson began measuring ozone concentrations in the atmosphere using a device known as a spectrophotometer. Meteorologists coined the term *Dobson units* (Du) to refer to the amount of ozone in the atmosphere. A typical ozone value is 300 Du.

Scientists first noticed an ozone "hole" in the late 1970s, which has become progressively larger over time. It's not a true hole but an area of severely depleted ozone where the concentration is less than 220 Du. It occurs each year between September and November over Antarctica, and up to 60 percent of the normally occurring ozone can be depleted in the deepest holes. When ozone is depleted more UVB radiation reaches earth. This leads to an increase in skin cancer in people and animals, which is, of course, a major concern.

DAMAGING CHEMICALS
Although the amount of ozone over the polar regions fluctuates naturally, scientists believe that it's primarily human activities that have reduced the amount of ozone in the stratosphere. The chemicals that cause the greatest damage to the ozone layer contain such elements as chlorine, fluorine, and bromine. Chlorofluorocarbons (CFCs) are the most notorious and damaging of these compounds. These synthetic chemicals were, until the mid-1990s, heavily used in many areas such as refrigeration, air-conditioning, cleaning, foam blowing, and as propellants in aerosol cans and fire extinguishers.

Recognizing the damage these chemicals cause, countries around the world are replacing them with more ozone-friendly substitutes. Although this is a step in the right direction, scientists don't expect the ozone layer to recover until at least 2050. Until then there will be an increase in skin-cancer rates in people and animals, along with damage to the tiny organisms that are the beginning of the food chain in Antarctic waters.

BELOW: This image of the Southern Hemisphere's ozone concentrations was taken by a TIROS satellite on October 6, 1996. Colors assigned by the computer to represent the ozone "hole" are gray (less than 100 Du) and red, crimson, and purple (210–100 Du). Other colors represent higher levels of ozone.

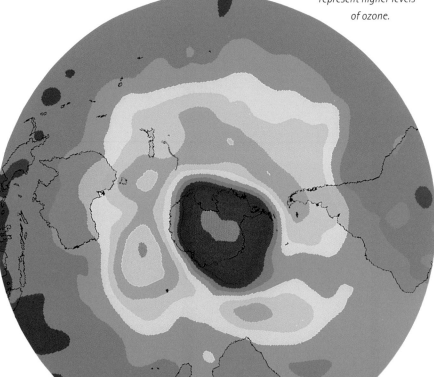

LEFT AND ABOVE: *This series of color-enhanced satellite maps shows the ozone "hole" over Antarctica in 1987, top left; 1988, top right; 1989, above left; and 1990, above right. The computer has assigned shades of pink and red to represent the "hole," which was smaller in 1988.*

RIGHT: *An ozone-research balloon is here being launched from the United States base at McMurdo, Antarctica. The balloon will take sensitive ozone-monitoring instruments tens of miles up into the stratosphere.*

ACID RAIN AND POLLUTION

Acid rain, nuclear accidents, and oil spills: these are all chilling reminders of how the human race has spoiled huge parts of the earth's fragile environment. Every day many millions of people worldwide live in heavily polluted cities. In the United States alone air pollution causes health problems that cost tens of billions of dollars annually. How bad the air pollution is and what happens to it are, of course, intimately linked to the weather.

ACID FROM THE SKY

In the 1970s scientists in several European countries noticed that the forests were dying and that fish stocks in lakes were dwindling at alarming rates. North America soon began to see similar ill effects, and by the mid-1990s some rapidly growing Asian countries were noticing them, too. Scientists found increasing acidity in water to be the cause and coined the term *acid rain*.

Air pollution is generated by industry, automobiles, coal-fired power stations, aircraft, and household activities, such as burning coal and wood for heat. Rain is an excellent cleanser of air that has been polluted by such chemicals as sulfur dioxide, nitrous oxide, ozone, lead, and a range of aerosols and particulates (minute particles). The combination of water and sulfur dioxide produces sulfuric acid, and water and nitrogen oxides make nitric acid. So rain, snow, fog, or dew forming in polluted air becomes mildly acidic.

Acid rain and acid deposited directly from air pollution affect all forms of life. They increase the acidity of vegetation, soil, rivers,

and lakes, which in turn contaminates water supplies, destroys vital nutrients in the soil, and poisons many small animals in the food chain.

To reduce the problem of acid rain, most countries in Europe and North America instituted very strict air-pollution reduction programs. By the mid-1990s there were encouraging signs that these measures were working. Acid levels were starting to fall and fish were returning to previously contaminated waterways. Some badly affected forests were also beginning to grow back.

URBAN WEATHER

Local weather can strongly influence how badly urban areas will be affected by smog and air pollution. Some of the worst affected places are cities located between the coast and a mountain range, such as Los Angeles and San Francisco in the United States, and Sydney and Perth in Australia. Land and sea breezes cause the pollution to drift out over the ocean at night and circle back over the city during the day, sometimes for days on end.

ENVIRONMENTAL DISASTERS

In 1986 radiation from an accident at the Chernobyl nuclear reactor, in the former Soviet Union, was dispersed by the wind across much of Eastern and Central Europe. The first the public knew of the accident was when monitoring stations in Finland, several hundred miles away, picked up the high levels of radiation. Similarly in 1989 wind and ocean currents dispersed millions of gallons of crude oil from the *Exxon Valdez* spill over a large area near the Alaskan coast. In both cases, knowledge of prevailing weather conditions was vital in reducing the impact of these toxic disasters.

Using information about the previous days' weather, the Finns were able to pinpoint the origin and path of the radiation before the Soviet government even released details about the accident. This allowed contaminated produce to be withdrawn from markets in time. Likewise, the *Exxon Valdez* pollution could have been much worse without advance knowledge of expected wind changes, which allowed many sensitive areas to be protected.

TOP: *Dead trees in the Czech Republic, killed by acid rain, stand as stark reminders of the large industrial zone in the background, which no doubt was the main cause of the acid rain.*

LEFT: *Automobiles are a major contributor to air pollution. Using a vehicle is the most polluting daily activity that people can do.*

ABOVE: *Extensive pollution from heavy industry is a major threat to the health of people and the environment around the world.*

RIGHT: *When moist, polluted air is exposed to sunlight it can form a choking blanket of brown, photochemical smog. Here, only the tallest buildings manage to peer through the smog shrouding New York City.*

HOW WEATHER AFFECTS PEOPLE

It's 120°F (49°C) in the shade, if you can find any, and a dust storm rages. Or it's 76°F below zero (−60°C), with a blizzard so severe you can barely see your hand in front of your face. Both conditions will kill an unprepared person within the hour, yet people have found ways to thrive in these, the harshest of weather conditions.

HOT AND COLD CLIMES
Whether it's the sandy deserts of Arabia and the Sahara, the cactus-dotted deserts of the southern United States and Mexico, or the

LEFT: People survive through the long northern winters by creating comfortable micro-climates for themselves and adjusting their diet. Buildings are designed to shed snow from their roofs, and to minimize heat loss. When working or traveling out of doors, the body must be protected from frostbite and hypothermia, which can kill.

ABOVE: For these herders and their reindeer, daily life in Arctic Russia during winter means coping with extreme cold. The reindeer have to find food either beneath the snow or by browsing on limited supplies of evergreen trees and shrubs.

spinifex plains of Central Australia, the key to survival is finding water and shelter from the heat. Traditionally nomadic tribes such as the Bedouin of Arabia move from one source of water to another. They travel in the early morning or evening, when it's cooler, and rest in the heat of the afternoon.

In hot, arid areas such as these, wearing loose, light-colored clothing keeps people cool by allowing air to circulate freely and reflecting heat. Arabs drape their traditional headdress, called *gutra*, across the face to keep out the hot

desert sand. Many Central American peoples wear broad-rimmed hats called sombreros to protect them from the sun's radiation.

People who live in cold climates, such as the Inuit, Russians, and Scandinavians, all know the value of thick, fur-lined clothing, which insulates them from extreme cold. In earlier times, people's ability to light fires helped to ensure their survival. Today sturdy, well-insulated housing, central heating, and heated motor vehicles allow people to live very comfortably despite the extreme cold.

FEELING SAD

From helping to spread diseases to making people feel depressed, the weather is a significant influence on people's well-being. Hot, humid conditions allow mosquito-borne diseases such as malaria to thrive because mosquitoes need these conditions to breed. Persistent, damp conditions favor the growth of molds, and mold spores can make asthma and other respiratory conditions worse. Dry, windy conditions stir up dust and blow pollen around, which may also trigger asthma or allergies, such as hayfever.

Some of the most common ailments are affected by the weather. People who suffer from arthritis commonly experience more pain in cold, damp weather, partly because the cold makes muscles contract over arthritic joints. Some people say that pain in the joints is often a reliable sign that storms are on the way. Doctors don't fully understand the reason for this, but one theory is that the sudden drop in air pressure before a storm causes the fluids in the joints to expand, which increases pain.

When the long, dark nights of winter arrive in countries in high latitudes, doctors have noticed that many more people become depressed and the suicide rate rises. This phenomenon has been called seasonal affective disorder, or SAD. The time between the dry and wet seasons in the tropics when the humidity builds up has also been found to cause an increase in depression. Once the monsoon has arrived, though, people's depression usually lifts.

GETTING USED TO THE WEATHER

Athletes who compete in different parts of the world have learned to allow time for their bodies to adjust to local weather conditions. If they are competing in events held well above sea level, for example, they will need to prepare themselves to perform with less oxygen, as was the case in the 1968 Mexico City Olympics. In the 1996 Atlanta Olympics the high levels of humidity meant athletes' bodies heated up more rapidly than usual. To escape the heat and humidity of the afternoon, and so avoid heat stress, the marathon was started at sunrise.

ABOVE: Floods created this scene of devastation in the San Fernando Valley, in California, leaving vehicles bogged in a sea of mud.

LEFT: This person is battling snow and icy winds on the streets of New York City.

ABOVE: *Even Batman would find the going difficult in these floodwaters in Vaison la Romaine, France.*

ABOVE RIGHT: *The beach is the place to cool off when the weather's hot, as these people in Brazil would agree. But staying out in the sun too long can lead to heat stress and sunburn.*

RIGHT: *Loose clothing and fabric draped across the face help protect this Berber man from the heat and sand. In desert regions the scarcity of water means that people have to move from oasis to oasis to survive.*

WEATHER AND WAR

Throughout history great military commanders have had to battle not only the enemy but also harsh and variable weather conditions. Some were able to adapt their battle plans to capitalize on the weather conditions. But for others bad weather spelled their doom.

STORMS AFOOT

In an ambitious attempt to conquer the Roman Empire in 218 BC, the Carthaginian general Hannibal led a force of 40,000 warriors, some on elephant-back, into the snow-clad European Alps. Although Hannibal survived the crossing, the loss of some 14,000 warriors in blizzards weakened his force so much that he was forced to abandon his Roman campaign.

A change in tactics in the Hundred Years' War (1337–1453) between England and France followed the Battle of Crécy, fought in 1346. The English forces were outnumbered three to one. Realizing rain would make the ground difficult to fight on, King Edward III of England organized his long-bowmen into an arc above an area of marshy ground. Immediately before the French attacked, there was a short but violent thunderstorm. The heavily armored French knights charged the English soldiers on horseback, only to become caught in the now muddy swamp, where they died in volley after volley of English arrows. From that point on French soldiers were no longer heavily armored.

TWO WORLD WARS

During World War I (1914–18) the introduction into the battlefield of aircraft, submarines, tanks, and mustard gas meant that it was crucial for weather-forecasting techniques to be accurate. In general, aircraft could fly only in fair weather, and many planes were unable to return to their home base because of strong head winds or deteriorating weather. In the fiercest storms in the North Atlantic Ocean, submarines were unable to launch their torpedoes, and poor visibility hampered both sides. On the Western Front mustard gas could be used only in cool conditions with light winds—even gentle breezes could blow the gas back onto the attacking forces.

During World War II (1939–45) German Field Marshal Rommel rose to fame because of his exploits in the North African deserts in 1942. Aware of the aerial supremacy of the Allies (the United States, Britain, and France), Rommel staged many of his most successful campaigns under the cover of dust storms, when the Allied aircraft were grounded.

During the height of the 1942–43 winter Adolf Hitler's decision to continue to advance his German forces on the Eastern Front against the Russian Army was seen as a significant tactical error. The Russians were used to the cold weather and used this period to mount a major offensive against the German Army, which lost a large number of experienced soldiers as well as the tactical advantage it had held until then.

THE GULF WAR

The Gulf War, triggered by the Iraqi invasion of Kuwait in August 1990, was a conflict where there was serious concern about the possible widespread use of chemical, biological, and even nuclear weapons in the battlefield. The weather played a large part in how the war unfolded. For example, no army could afford to use chemical or biological weapons near the battlefront unless it was confident that the chemicals or biological agent would not blow back on its own forces.

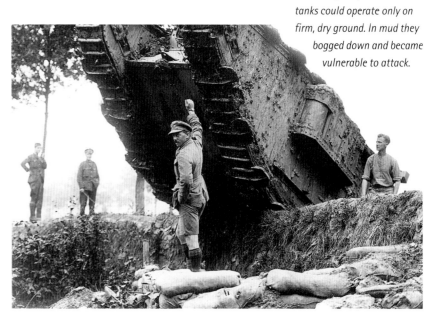

BELOW: Ungainly World War I tanks could operate only on firm, dry ground. In mud they bogged down and became vulnerable to attack.

ABOVE: *Heat, wind, and dust are additional enemies in desert warfare. Military strategists used weather predictions to reduce the risks to their ground troops, such as these foot soldiers in a southern Iraqi desert during the Gulf War.*

BELOW: Although Hannibal went on to win three important battles in Italy, the loss of so many warriors in the fierce Alpine blizzards eventually forced him to abandon his campaign to conquer the Roman Empire.

RIGHT: Aircraft fighting air battles in World War I, such as the German triplanes depicted here, needed favorable weather conditions to allow them to find their way home safely.

WHAT DOES THE FUTURE HOLD?

Few things are certain, but what *is* certain is that the world's population will continue to grow rapidly in the future. When massive storms such as hurricanes occur, more people will be affected by the devastation this extreme weather brings, and the damage will be much more expensive to repair. However, because of improvements in the way they monitor weather, meteorologists will be better able to predict new weather extremes. As demand for finite food resources becomes acute, we will need to make informed decisions based on the predicted future weather.

WEATHER IN CYBERSPACE

The 21st century will be the information age. In the early 1990s people had to rely on newspapers, television, and radio reports for information about the weather. Today more and more people are gaining access to weather reports on the Internet, and mobile-phone systems will soon have uninterrupted global coverage. These new and expanded communication methods have opened up an enormous source of highly varied weather information, whenever and wherever it's needed.

By the mid-1990s all major national weather services and meteorological research agencies had set up home pages on the World Wide Web (WWW), and many individuals had produced their own weather pages on the Net. Today global "weather chat" groups are well established, and e-mail lists for those with similar interests are common.

Education on the environment and weather is already part of the Web. A project called GLOBE (Global Learning and Observations to Benefit the Environment) links 3,000 schools in 48 countries, as they explore the global environment and exchange weather and environmental information. Initiatives such as these mark the advent of universally accessible, up-to-the-minute information on the latest weather observations, forecasts, and research.

ABOVE: *Technicians work on the European weather satellite Meteosat at Aerospatiale, France. This is one of the newest generation of geosynchronous satellites placed into orbit above the Equator. They keep up with the rotation of the earth, taking precisely 24 hours for each orbit. They continuously survey the weather thousands of miles below.*

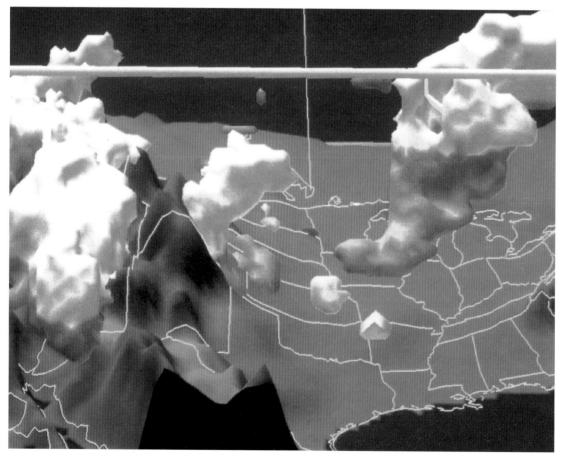

LEFT: *A virtual-reality weather display developed by the Forecast Systems Laboratory in Boulder, Colorado, for the aviation industry. The pink areas show regions of the atmosphere where there is a potential icing hazard to aircraft over the central United States. The background is an exaggerated depiction of the terrain. The red areas represent a typical cruising level for commercial aircraft. Displays such as this one can be manipulated by navigators and pilots so they can see from any angle what kind of weather is occurring, reducing the likelihood of flying in hazardous weather.*

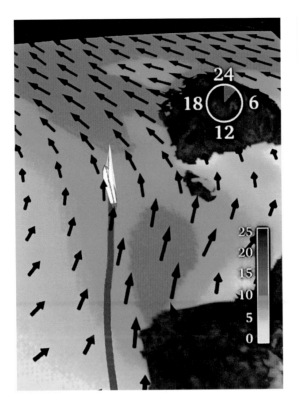

RIGHT: A snapshot of a three-dimensional animation of the record-breaking yacht Morning Glory *sailing to victory in Australia's 1996 Sydney-to-Hobart Yacht Race. A high-resolution numerical model (see page 126) has been used to calculate the predicted wind field, which is represented by the colored background. The colored bar represents wind speed in knots.*

FAR RIGHT: A computer graphic showing a fractal image from the Mandelbrot set. Fractals were first described in mathematical terms by Polish-born French mathematician Benoît B. Mandelbrot. They are used to explain complex natural structures, such as snowflakes and clouds. They may, in the future, help to unravel some of the complexities of weather.

Weather services and universities are fast becoming able to feed information from global mathematical weather models (see page 126) into very small-scale models on laptop computers via the Internet. This will allow people in remote places, such as farmers on isolated ranches and sailors on the open seas, to access their very own detailed weather forecasts, whenever and wherever they need them.

VIRTUAL REALITY

As a way of gaining information, the written word continues to serve us well in many areas, but it does have immense limitations, considering the huge range of languages and dialects in use in the world. These days, written reports on the current and future weather are being replaced by self-explanatory images and multimedia representations, such as virtual reality (three-dimensional animation).

The next generation of weather satellites, specialized weather surveillance radar, and large networks of automatic weather stations and wind profilers (instruments that continuously measure the wind speed and direction for several miles above the ground) will produce a bewildering volume of data. However, as computers become more powerful, and as more and more people gain access to the WWW, many weather services are turning to numerical data and satellite images to produce three-dimensional animated pictures of the weather on television and the Net—a virtual reality that almost everyone can appreciate.

THE SCIENCE OF WEATHER

Advances in technology also mean that mathematical models are becoming more complex. Together with improvements in scientists' understanding of chaos and uncertainty in the atmosphere, these models will allow meteorologists to forecast the weather with greater accuracy from minutes to several decades ahead.

Soon computers will automatically perform the more routine tasks of the weather forecaster. Meteorologists will use computers more intensively to analyze the steadily increasing stream of data, enabling them to identify features that trigger significant weather. Tomorrow's weather will hold fewer surprises as computers become faster and smarter.

INDEX

CONTRIBUTORS AND PICTURE CREDITS

CONTRIBUTORS

BRUCE BUCKLEY is deputy officer-in-charge of the Australian Bureau of Meteorology's New South Wales office. His duties span meteorological observations, engineering, and computing support for bureau activities throughout NSW. He worked in Saudi Arabia from 1987–91 with the national Meteorological and Environmental Protection Administration.

JOHN R. COLQUHOUN works for the Australian Bureau of Meteorology's forecasting services in New South Wales, including general services to the public and special services to aviation and defense. He has published several research papers on thunderstorm forecasting and tornadoes in United States journals.

PAT SULLIVAN has been in charge of the Australian Bureau of Meteorology's New South Wales office since 1982. Previous appointments include being senior meteorologist in the World Weather Watch Centre, Melbourne, and weather forecasting in Tasmania. From 1987–90, he lead an Australian team working in Saudi Arabia with the national Meteorological and Environmental Protection Administration.

RICHARD WHITAKER manages the Australian Bureau of Meteorology's commercial meteorological activities in New South Wales. He was formerly senior forecaster at the Sydney Forecasting Centre, and weather forecaster at Sydney International Airport. He was a consultant editor and co-author of *The Nature Company Guides: Weather*.

PHOTOGRAPHIC CREDITS

AKG = AKG Photo, London; APL = Australian Picture Library; Auscape = Auscape International; BCL = Bruce Coleman Ltd; Bridgeman = The Bridgeman Art Library; FLPA = Frank Lane Picture Agency; IPL = International Photographic Library; PM = Picture Media; TIB = The Image Bank; TPL = The Photo Library, Sydney; TSA = Tom Stack and Associates
t = top, b = bottom, l = left, r = right, c = center, i = inset, b/g = background

front jacket Keith Kent/TPL/SPL **back jacket** Jeff Foott/Auscape **i** TIB/ITTC Productions **1** J Brandenburg/Minden Pictures/APL **2** John Perret/TPL **3** John Shaw/BCL **6–7** Paul van Gaalen/BCL **7i** John Shaw/BCL **8** Avril Makula **9b/g** David R Frazier/TPL; **li** Jeff Foott Productions/ BCL; **ri** Darrell Gulin/TPL **10t** NASA/SPL/TPL **10–11b** Nicholas de Vore/BCL **11tl** Dries van Zyl/BCL **12b** Tony Craddock/TPL **12–13br** David Miller **15tl** Bob and Clara Calhoun/ BCL; **tr** Avril Makula; **bl** Linde Waidhofer/ Liaison International/ Wildlight Photo Agency; **br** John Shaw/BCL **16t** Baum and Hembest/SPL/TPL; **c** Baum and Hembest/SPL/TPL **17tl** NASA; **br** Steven C Kaufman/BCL **18t** Ted Mead/TPL; **b** Mr Jules Cowan/BCL **19t** Johnny Johnson/BCL **20b** Luiz Claudio Marigo/BCL; **tr** Giraudon **21t** Bob and Clara Calhoun/BCL **23** Erwin and Peggy Bauer/BCL **24–5bc** NASA/SPL/TPL **25br** Giorgio Gualco/BCL **26** IPL **27t** Mr Jules Cowan/BCL; **i** ESA/TSADO/TSA **28** Thomas Buchholz/BCL **29** AT Willett/TIB **30–1b** Eric and David Hosking/ FLPA **31t** Eric and David Hosking/FLPA **32br** Dr Hermann Brehm/BCL **32–3c** F

Polking/FLPA **33r** John Shaw/BCL **34** Geoff Dore/BCL **35** IPL **37b** GSFC/TSADO/TSA **38–9** Randy Wells/TPL **39i** Richard Kaylin/TPL **40tl** Gary Braasch; **tr** Bullaty Lomeo/TIB **41t** Nicholas Parfitt/TPL **42tr** Dr Sabine M Schmidt/BCL **43c** Allan G Potts/BCL; **l** Allan G Potts/BCL **44t** Kevin Rushby/BCL **45t** Jeff Foott Productions/BCL **46tl** Zefa/APL **47** Horizon Photo Library **48l** Peter Jarver **48–9t** Pete Turner/ TIB **49b** Peter Jarver **51b/g** Keith Kent/SPL/TPL; **l** John Cancalosi/BCL **52t** Siegfried Eigstler/TPL; **cr** Colin Varndell/BCL **53t** Ted Mead/TPL **54t** Avril Makula; **b** Levy/Gamma Liaison/PM **55tD** Dugan/FLPA; **bl** Avril Makula; **br** Jeff Foott Productions/ BCL **57l** Liz Hymans/TPL; **tr** Pekka Parviainen/SPL/TPL; **cr** David Miller; **br** Erik Bjurstrom/BCL **58–9** IPL **59i** Michael Klinec/BCL **60t** IPL; **b** Alain Compost/BCL **61** Dr SB Idso/FLPA **62–3b** Eric Meola/TIB **63tl** Keister/Gamma Liaison/PM **64t** NASA/SPL/TPL **65bl** Jocelyn Burt/TPL; **t** Peter Solness **66–7c** Tony Bee/TPL **68b** Larry Lipsky/ TSA **69t** SPL/TPL; **cl** NOAA/SPL/TPL **70–1** Steve McCurry/Magnum Photos **71r** Steve McCurry/Magnum Photos **72t** Robert McLeod/Robert Harding Picture Library **73t** John Carnemolla/APL; **b** Pacific Stock/APL **74–5c** Jeff Foott/BCL **75b** Hank Morgan/SPL/TPL **76–7** Richard Kaylin/TPL **77i** David Miller **80t** Peter A Hinchliffe/BCL ; **b** J Sorensen and J Olsen/NHPA; **81t** Geoff Higgins/ TPL; **b** Peter A Hinchliffe/BCL **82t** Oasis Inc./BCL; **b** Norbert Schwirtz/BCL **83t** David Miller; **b** Bill Bachman **84t** J Szkodzinski/TIB; **b** Peter Jarver **85** Peter Jarver **86t** Peter Jarver; **b** Bob Wickham/TPL **87t** Maurice Nimmo/FLPA; **b** Johnny Johnson/BCL **88t** Darryl Torckler/TPL; **b** Richard Myers/National Centre for Atmospheric Research **89** Gary Braasch **90t** Peter Jarver; **b** Avril Makula **91t** Avril Makula; **b** B Stone/FLPA **92t** Peter Jarver; **b** AT Willett/TIB **93t** AT Willett/TIB; **b** H Hoflinger/ FLPA **94t** B. Wisser/Gamma Liaison/PM; **b** Gary Hansen/Auscape **95t** Peter Jarver; **b** Olivier Martel/ Black Star/Headpress **96t** Steve Krongard/TIB; **b** P Parvianinen/FLPA **97t** and **b** Gary Braasch **98t** Fred Bruemmer/BCL; **b** Dr Scott Nielsen/BCL **99t** Pekka Parviainen/SPL/TPL; **b** Peter Turner **100–1** Terry Donnelly/TSA **101i** W. Wisniewski/FLPA **102b** Frans Lemens/TIB **102–3c** Jules Cowan/BCL **103bl** Brian Parker/TSA; **br** Koos Delport/FLPA **104tl** M. Newman/FLPA; **tr** Gary Milburn/TSA; **bl** Gary Milburn/TSA **105** Brett Baunton/TPL; **i** Janos Jurka/BCL **106v** David Hosking/FLPA; **b** Fred Bruemmer/BCL **107t** MPL Fogden/BCL; **b** Gary Milburn/TSA; **108t** Jean-Paul Nacivet/TPL; **bl** John Shaw/NHPA; **br** Paul van Gaalen/BCL **109t** Jens Rydell/BCL **110t** Johnny Johnson/BCL; **b** Dr Eckart Pott/BCL **111tl** Staffan Widstrand/BCL; **tr** W. Wisniewski/FLPA; **b** Johnny Johnson/BCL **112–13** Michael Busselle/TPL **113i** SPL/TPL **114t** Wayne Lankinen/BCL; **bl** Stephen Dalton/NHPA; **br** Bernard Roussel/TIB **115t** David Miller **116t** Biblioteca Nazionale Centrale, Florence/Bridgeman **117tl** Provincial Museum, Victoria, BC/Werner Forman Archive; **tr** Royal Library, Copenhagen/Bridgeman; **b** British Museum/AKG Photo **118b** Scott Polar Research Institute,

Cambridge/Bridgeman **119** P. Crescenzi, Le Rusticana Chantilly, Musée Condé/AKG **120 tl** Musée du Louvre/AKG; **tr** Royal Naval College, Greenwich/Bridgeman; **bl** Jean-Loup Charmet; **br** AKG **121** Private Collection/ Bridgeman **122t** Mike Langford/Auscape **123b/g** SPL/TPL; **i** NASA/SPL/TPL **124** Stephen Krasemann/NHPA **125tl & tr** Peter Jarver; **b** D. Parer and E. Parer-Cook/Auscape **126** David Parker/SPL/TPL **127t** National Center for Atmospheric Research; **c** Bill Bachman; **b** Levy/Gamma Liaison/PM **128** David Parker/SPL/TPL **129t** John Lund/TPL; **cl** Paul Nevin/TPL; **cr** David Parker/SPL/TPL **131bg** John Shaw/BCL; **i** Michael Melford **132t** Peter Knowles/TPL; **bl** TPL; **br** NBC Press **133tl** Earth Satellite Corp/TPL; **tr** Swersey/Liaison/PM **134** Oliver Strewe **135** Australian Geographic **136–7** Flip Chalfant/TIB **137i** TPL **138t** Tui de Roy/Auscape; **b** Andrew J. Martinez/TPL; **cr** Eckart Pott/BCL **139tl** Tom Till/Auscape **140l** Ted Mead/TPL **140–1r** Jacques Jangoux/TPL **142t** Guido Alberto Rossi/TIB **143t** Grant V. Faint/TIB **144b** NOAA/ SPL/TPL **144–5tc** NASA/SPL/TPL **145r** Galen Rowell/TPL **146bl** Gary Braasch **146–7c** TPL; **tc** Simon Fraser/SPL/TPL **147r** AP **148b** Janos Jurka/ BCL **148–9t** Staffan Widstrand/BCL **150t** LA Daily News/Gamma Liaison/PM; **b** Swersey/Gamma Liaison/PM **151tl** François Lochon/Gamma/PM; **tr** Andy Caulfield/TIB; **b** Harald Lange/BCL **152br** AKG **152–3t** AAP **153b & tr** AKG **154t** David Parker/TPL **155tl** VisLab, Sydney **155tr** Alfred Pasieka/TPL

ILLUSTRATION CREDITS

Nick Farmer/Brihton Illustration: 27, 30, 40, 46, 52, 53, 65
Chris Forsey: 11, 14, 17, 22, 28, 29, 36, 42, 48, 50, 56, 63, 68; maps 19, 36, 37, 71
Robert Hynes: 12, 24, 44, 45
Rod Westblade: map 71

CAPTIONS

1 A rainbow in Alberta, Canada.
2 Dense storm clouds over Western Australia.
3 Dunes and cottonwood trees in Great Sand Dunes National Monument, Colorado.
6–7 Frost-covered willow trees in winter, Holland. Inset: Spring flowers on the Texas prairie.
38–9 Cumulus clouds above a rapeseed field. Inset: Lightning over Colorado.
58–9 A waterspout off the coast of southern Italy. Inset: A windmill in Sjaelland, Denmark.
76–7 Lightning striking an electricity pylon, Nevada. Inset: The rising sun.
100–1 Bigelow cholla cactus, chuparosa, and brittlebrush in Plum Canyon, Anza-Borrego Desert State Park, California. Inset: Emperor penguin with young, Atka Bay, Weddell Sea, Antarctica.
112–13 Tree in wheat field. Inset: Color satellite image of severe storm in Bering Sea.
136–7 White water park, Marietta, Atlanta, Georgia. Inset: People in the rain.

ACKNOWLEDGMENTS

The publishers wish to thank the following people for their assistance in the production of this book: Lynn Cole, Edan Corkill and Robert Coupe.